"Want to be blessed? Many of us believe if we work hard and succeed, we will be. But my friend Alan Wright explains how that's totally backwards! The blessing isn't a reward for productivity but the fuel for it. This book will not only inspire you but give practical instructions to speak a blessing over others. I recommend it!"

Eric Metaxas, #1 *New York Times* bestselling author;
host of the nationally syndicated *Eric Metaxas Radio Show*

"What a wonderful and refreshing book! Not only will this book offer a practical and powerful way to give blessing to others, it will bless you. If you've ever struggled with shame, pretense, loneliness, or drift (and I do), get ready to be blessed and to bless others."

Steve Brown, radio teacher; seminary professor;
author of numerous books, including *Talk the Walk*

"I'm thrilled that Alan Wright is putting this great truth of blessing in the context of the gospel. Understanding the privilege we're given to put words to the truth of Jesus's finished work is so life-giving. We are blessed to be able to bless."

Dudley Hall, popular conference speaker;
author of numerous books, including *Grace Works*

"In a season when so many people crave life-giving words, Alan's book is a call to speak blessing and watch as lives change. We are meant to give blessings, not just receive them, so let's begin speaking the words the world needs to hear."

Josh Surratt, lead pastor, Seacoast Church, Mount Pleasant, SC

"Every spouse, parent, teacher, boss, and coach needs to read this book. Yes, hurt people may hurt people, but Pastor Alan brilliantly shows us how blessed people bless people—by the transforming power of the gospel!"

Stu Epperson Jr., author of *Last Words of Jesus*;
president and host, The Truth Network

"In the Bible there's a hidden principle that can be called 'blessing by association,' which is the reality of being verbally, prayerfully, and practically charged by others to succeed. It is far more powerful than merely wishing someone well. Pastor Alan unlocks this divine asset. Just as physical wealth or poverty is transferred from one generation to the next, spoken blessings can also transfer spiritual wealth to the next generation!"

Rufus Smith, senior pastor, Hope Evangelical
Presbyterian Church, Memphis, TN

"Alan is a creative communicator and storyteller for whom words are like paint colors on an artist's brush. He's insightful, funny, tender, and deep. This book fed my brain and my heart. Sometimes I found myself intellectually delighted while simultaneously tearing up. Alan helps us see and feel the power of blessing."

David Dwight, senior pastor, Hope Church, Richmond, VA;
author of *Start Here*

"With so many people living through an epidemic of inferiority, one caused by a secular view of self instead of a biblical one, *The Power to Bless* solidifies the foundation on which we ought to stand. Alan Wright has given us an inspiring, accessible, and practical work to help us change our approach both to self and to others."

David Swanson, senior pastor, First Presbyterian Church
of Orlando; author of *Everlasting Life*
and *Learning to Be You*

"Alan Wright's newest book, *The Power to Bless*, is a breath of fresh air for discouraged and disheartened people. His insight on the hidden potential residing in each person is the perfect prescription to inject new life and hope into weary hearts. You have a treasure hidden deep within you—a tangible glory to manifest God's divine purpose for your life."

Bishop J.C. Hash, senior pastor, St. Peter's World Outreach
Center, Winston-Salem, NC; author of *Listening Prayer*

"If we can only learn to bless and empower others as this book teaches, we will see real changes happening in homes, churches, and the lives of those we love."

Sam Chelladurai, senior pastor, AFT Church,
Chennai, India; Bible College founder

THE
POWER TO
BLESS

THE POWER TO
BLESS

How to Speak Life and
Empower the People You Love

ALAN WRIGHT

BakerBooks
a division of Baker Publishing Group
Grand Rapids, Michigan

Published by Baker Books
a division of Baker Publishing Group
PO Box 6287, Grand Rapids, MI 49516-6287
www.bakerbooks.com

Printed in the United States of America

Library of Congress Cataloging-in-Publication Data
Names: Wright, Alan, 1962– author.
Title: The power to bless : how to speak life and empower the people you love / Alan
    Wright.
Description: Grand Rapids, Michigan : Baker Books, a division of Baker Publishing
    Group, 2021.
Identifiers: LCCN 2020024594 | ISBN 9781540900555 (cloth)
Subjects: LCSH: Blessing and cursing. | Benediction. | Ephraim (Tribe of Israel) |
    Manasseh (Tribe of Israel)
Classification: LCC BV4520 .W745 2021 | DDC 242/.7—dc23
LC record available at https://lccn.loc.gov/2020024594

Some names and identifying details have been changed to protect the privacy of individuals.

The author is represented by Alive Literary Agency, www.aliveliterary .com.

21 22 23 24 25 26 27   7 6 5 4 3 2 1

green press
INITIATIVE

For Dudley Hall,
my spiritual father

Contents

PART THREE   Giving the Blessing

Foreword

Too many times we "kill" the people who are closest to us by harsh, cruel words. Many homes could be turned from a morgue to a home of life if we would change words of death to words of life. This book will help you do that.

For most of us in the Western world, the concept of verbally blessing another person is not on our radar—unless you live in the southern United States, where people regularly say, "Bless your heart, honey." But blessing is more than empathizing with someone who has shared a personal difficulty. Most of the time, if we use the word *blessing* at all, we think in terms of supplying the physical needs of someone—like providing money to pay their rent to keep them from being evicted. Caring for others is wonderful, but the biblical idea of blessing others is deeper than merely helping others with their tangible needs.

When Christians think of the word *blessed*, our minds turn to what we commonly call Jesus's Sermon on the Mount. In it He spoke of the blessing that would come to certain groups of people: the poor in spirit, those who mourn, the meek, those who hunger and thirst for righteousness, the merciful, the pure in heart, the peacemakers, and those who are persecuted because of righteousness (Matt. 5:1–10). Jesus pronounced a blessing upon each of these. It was related to their specific need. He clearly predicted that something good would happen to all these people. In this sense, all Christians are greatly blessed in many ways. Most amazing of all is that God has given to us what we don't deserve—eternal life in His presence.

However, I find few Christians who have dug deeply into the Hebrew concept of fathers giving a verbal blessing to their children or grandchildren. Nor do I often hear one Christian giving a verbal blessing to another. Yet this concept is deeply embedded in Scripture. In *The Power to Bless*, Alan Wright gives insights into this biblical practice. Because I've known Alan for many years, I know this isn't simply a theological study. The giving of verbal blessings to his children, his congregation, and others is a practice he has personally implemented for the past twenty-five years.

Many of us have underestimated the powerful influence of a verbal blessing. Yet the Scriptures say, "The tongue has the power of life and death, and those who love it will eat its fruit" (Prov. 18:21 NIV). I believe that every Christian could leave a legacy of life if we implemented the practice of giving verbal blessings to others.

Gary Chapman, PhD, author of *The 5 Love Languages*

Many Thanks

Anne, my love—it would have been better if, instead of writing a book on the power to bless, I could have just shown the whole world you in action.

Bennett—every day you fulfill your name. You are, in a word, a blessing.

Abby, "her father's joy"—your fingerprints are on this manuscript, and your touch is deft.

Amy, my beloved daughter-in-law—our world became much brighter when you stepped into it. Much.

My remarkable mother—thank you for leading me to the Father of all blessing.

Reynolda Church—after twenty-five years, I'm still in love with you. "Are you ready for some good news?"

Chris Lawson, my executive pastor—thank you for preaching, praying, believing, leading, and everything else you did to make this book (and my life) possible.

Laura Hull, my assistant—you are "the hub."

My team at Reynolda Church—it's so fun to work with friends.

The Alan Wright Ministries team: Jeff, Hugh, James, Bob, Cherrie, and Scott—thanks for helping so many see themselves in a whole new light.

My agent, Bryan Norman—I wish I could explain how much I enjoy every conversation with you.

My editor, Brian Vos—when you scored twenty-eight runs and took home a stuffed animal from the Myrtle Beach arcade, I knew I'd partnered with a winner.

Melanie Burkhardt, Mark Rice, Jessica English, Patti Brinks, Erin Bartels, Rachel O'Connor, Janelle Wiesen, Kelli Smith, Eileen Hanson, and the whole Baker Books team—your passion for good books makes glad the heart of God.

Introduction

The Blessing I Never Knew

Some people try hard to succeed so they will feel blessed. Other people try hard to succeed because they already feel blessed. It's the difference between striving and thriving. It's the difference between death and life.

For most of my life I was the former: laboring for the blessing I never knew.

By the time I turned forty, my father had quit his years of hard drinking, his physical health was on the upswing, and he seemed open to talking about it all. So my brothers and I had a few counseling sessions with the father I loved so much but knew so little.

"Dad," I said during our first session, "there's something I'd like from you. If you'd be willing, I think it would really help me."

"Sure," my father said. "What is it?"

"I'd like you to bless me."

My father didn't know what I meant. And the counselor didn't either.

"I mean it in the biblical sense," I explained. "I've been studying how Hebrew fathers blessed their children. Blessing isn't what you say before a meal or after someone sneezes. It's not a prayer either. I'm talking about an affirming, positive vision spoken with faith, love, and discernment over someone's life."

Dad had left home when I was in fourth grade, so he wasn't around to paint a positive vision for my future. Evidently, he bragged to others about me, but he wasn't comfortable looking me in the eye, affirming my unique gifts, and pointing me toward a God-given destiny. So I grew up trying to prove my value as I groped in the dark for my place in the world. Though some unblessed people rebel, I performed in order to feel blessed—make all A's, obey all the rules, win all the tennis matches. I was trying to buy blessing, but it was costing me joy and peace. I grew weary of trying to prove my worth. I hated feeling ashamed and anxious. But mostly, I knew I would never reach my potential until I was blessed.

At the next counseling session, my father brought three index cards on which he'd inscribed words of blessing for his three boys.

"Alan," he read, "when we brought you home from the hospital as a baby, your two-year-old brother Mark asked, 'Why'd we have to get *him*?'" We chuckled as Dad continued, "We now know it's because we would need you."

Dad's few words of blessing were morsels for a malnourished soul, and I gobbled them up like a starving person. My delight in my father's simple affirmation confirmed something I'd suspected from my study of God's Word: we crave blessing because we are designed for it.

Has anyone ever looked you in the eye, affirmed your infinite value, identified your unique gifts, and pointed you toward a God-given destiny? What would it mean to you for someone to speak that sort of positive vision in faith over your life?

Think about the people you love. Don't you long to help them grow and flourish? How might you impact their lives if you became skilled in the practice of blessing?

Here's my point: everyone needs to be blessed.

Without blessing, we will have no deep security and feel no real release from past failures. Unblessed, we'll never be as fruitful as God has planned, and we won't walk fully in the favor of God.

The Power of Blessing

Because my father was an eloquent, professional communicator, I wish he could have blessed me as a preacher, radio teacher, and writer.

My love for communicating started early. I remember my seventh grade English teacher not only because she was the prettiest teacher I ever had but also because she introduced me to public speaking. For some reason she thought it was important that we learn to prepare, practice, and deliver a speech as part of our English curriculum. All my buddies hated the assignment, but I loved it.

Later, someone introduced me to the Optimist Club speech contest in Greensboro, North Carolina. I competed against kids from around the region, giving a six-minute speech related to a current event of my choice. I spoke about the Charles Manson loyalist Squeaky Fromme, who, in 1975, attempted to assassinate President Gerald Ford.

I won the contest.

I wish my dad could've been there, because he was a college debate champion who became a pioneer in TV news investigative reporting and eventually won an Edward R. Murrow Award for broadcasting. He was brilliant. He could make a news story sing, and his on-air reporting was lyrical. But like the cobbler whose son had no shoes, my father filled the airwaves with his powerful words—never me.

I can only imagine what it would have done for me if Dad had seen me get the speech trophy and said, "Alan, wow, you have a real communication gift. That's going to be a great tool for you in life, Son." I think something mystical and wonderful would have happened to me. I didn't need the trophy nearly as much as I needed someone to interpret the award for me.

Where there is no blessing, there is no notice of God's grace or His plan. No vision emerges for the future. Without the blessing, life drifts. But when someone affirms your potential, you focus and become twice as fruitful.

I've seen the power of blessing up close. During her seventh grade year, our daughter, Abigail, told me about an assignment in her English course. She had to prepare and deliver a speech for her class and wanted my help. She was about the age I was when I won the Optimist Club speech contest. I sat on the blue couch in the living room as she stood a few feet away with her notes—a nervous, giggling middle school girl trying out her first speech for an audience of one.

Thirty seconds into it, I was amazed that her cadence was natural and her tone was warm. With no training, she exuded a persuasive confidence that made my soul stand at attention. She finished her speech, fumbled her notes, and blushed.

"Abby," I said, "you have a gift. God has given you a way with words that is convincing and inspiring. You speak naturally, eloquently, and powerfully. I can see you going far with this gift."

"Aw, Dad, did you really like it?"

My blessing was simple, but can you imagine the impact it had on Abby?

Have you ever felt so much affection for someone that you wished you could, by some sort of osmosis, deposit your goodwill into them? I felt that way the first time I held our first child. I knew that I would pray for that child every day and do everything possible to help him thrive in this world, but I wanted to do more. I yearned to partner with God for the impartation of strength and favor in his life.

Dallas Willard defined *blessing* as "the projection of good into the life of another. It isn't just words. It's the actual putting forth of your will for the good of another person."[1]

Who would you like to see flourish like that? A child? A parent? A friend? A coworker? If you haven't been blessing them, it's not too late. You can start today.

Two years after Abby's speech in the living room, she joined NCFCA, a national debate and speech organization that holds local, regional, and national competitions. She excelled immediately, made lifelong friends, and in tenth grade qualified for the national tournament held that year in Minneapolis. On the final night of the tournament, amid great fanfare in the large auditorium, the national director announced, "The 2015 After Dinner Speech national champion is Abby Wright!" Fifteen hundred of her peers and their families from around the nation gave her a standing ovation.

Does blessing make the difference between winning a local speech contest and succeeding on a national platform? Often, yes. But the power of blessing is about much more than accumulating trophies. It's about the deeper treasures of God's grace that last forever.

Blessing doesn't guarantee fame and fortune, but it does fuel the hope, expectancy, confidence, and hard work that often lead to success. Even at her tender age, Abby knew it wasn't just her skills that had brought her to that platform. She wasn't merely gifted—she was blessed.

Blessed people flourish by a power that transcends human talent or hard work. They have a mystical grace at work in their hearts that makes them effective and joyful. People who know they are blessed aren't struggling to prove their worth—they're confident of their value and sure they can make a difference in the world. That's why blessed people bless people. That's why blessed people don't feel helpless to help others.

It is therefore no surprise that the theme of blessing shapes the whole narrative of the Bible.

God blessed Adam and Eve to empower their productivity. He then formed a people for Himself by blessing Abraham and promising to bless the nations through him. As we'll see, the stories of Isaac, Jacob, Esau, and Joseph revolve around the power to bless. In accord with God's instructions to Moses, the priests regularly spoke blessing over the people. Leaders like David blessed their families. When Christ was born, Simeon appeared and blessed the baby and His family. Jesus began His ministry with a series of blessings called beatitudes, and His last act on earth was blessing: "While he blessed them, he parted from them and was carried up into heaven" (Luke 24:51).

Like a golden thread, the power of blessing weaves the Scriptures together, and in the Old Testament, one intriguing blessing stands out.

Israel's Most Important Family Blessing

For 3,700 years, Jewish dads have been speaking blessing to their children—pointing out a child's gifts or virtues and forecasting good things for the future. But for thousands of years, these fathers have started the blessing for their sons with the puzzling words "May God make you like Ephraim and Manasseh."

I've been to seminary and studied the Bible most of my life, but it wasn't until I started learning about the biblical concept of blessing that I paid any attention to Ephraim and Manasseh. They're Joseph's sons who were born to him in Egypt. They don't appear in any major scenes of the Old Testament narrative. They never say anything. None of their accomplishments are ever noted. So why, for thousands of years, have Jewish fathers been saying, "May God make you like Ephraim and Manasseh"? Why not "May God make you like Moses and Joshua" or "Elijah and Elisha" or "David and Solomon"?

The Scriptures mandate the Ephraim and Manasseh blessing. When Joseph's father, Jacob, was dying, Joseph rushed his boys to their grandfather's bedside for Jacob to bless them. What unfolded in those moments is mysterious and fascinating.

First, Jacob adopted his grandsons as his own. Then he crossed his arms and deliberately put his right hand on the head of the younger grandson, Ephraim, and his left hand on the firstborn, Manasseh. By doing this, Jacob violated all social norms. The firstborn always was entitled to the stronger blessing, symbolized by the right hand. But Jacob insisted on keeping his arms crossed and blessed his grandchildren, saying, "When a blessing is given in Israel, they will say: 'May God make you like Ephraim and Manasseh.' In this way he made Ephraim greater than Manasseh" (Gen. 48:20 NCV).

Though this powerful blessing has been announced for 3,700 years as arguably the most important blessing in the Old Testament, there's no consensus within Jewish scholarship about its purpose. So what is it about this blessing that makes it so important?

The Ephraim and Manasseh blessing is prominent and powerful because it reveals four essential gifts that God wants you to receive and share with others. Through the lens of this one all-important family blessing, you'll learn about the power, purpose, and practice of blessing. As you'll discover, the portrait of God's grace in the Ephraim and Manasseh story is awe-inspiring. When you see the picture in full, it takes your breath away.

In this book I want to do two things: impart this blessing to you and teach you how to bless others. The Ephraim and Manasseh story provides a proven plan to receive and share the essential gifts of biblical blessing:

1) *Security.* Blessing assures us that we are loved. When we know we are loved and wanted, we are secure and confident. When we're secure, we soar.
2) *Freedom.* Blessing releases us from the binding power of yesterday's pain. God wants us to live like we've forgotten all our troubles.
3) *Fruitfulness.* Blessing releases productivity. God made us to be fruitful, and His blessing can make us twice as fruitful as we ever imagined.
4) *Favor.* Blessing takes us beyond our limited skills and ambitions. God's favor opens doors for us that no amount of hard work ever could.

What would your life look like with these four gifts of the Ephraim and Manasseh blessing? Who do you want to bless so they can live that sort of abundant life?

You can see your spouse, your children, your friends, your coworkers, and even the difficult people in your life becoming all that God created them to be. Let's be clear: to be blessed doesn't mean that all your problems go away. But it does mean that you and those you bless can have more joy, eliminate negative thinking, embrace opportunities, and be filled with God's power.

After twenty-five years of teaching the concept and personally speaking blessing to thousands of individuals, I'm convinced that, other than God's work through prayer, blessing is the most powerful tool for change in the world. It's not magic. It's thoroughly biblical.

If you've missed the blessing from someone important in your life, don't give up. It's never too late. You'll find inspiration and blessing in the pages ahead.

If you wish you had blessed others more than you have, this book won't make you feel bad about it—it'll show you a new and better way. Unfortunately, blessing doesn't come naturally to most people. It's a skill you need to choose to learn. So I'll show you how to craft a biblical, life-empowering blessing using a simple, four-step process that I've been using for years. I've even developed a blessing worksheet that will guide you step-by-step.

Eight years after the day my father blessed me in the counselor's office, I held his hand at his skilled-care facility. Dad's breathing began slowing. I had known for weeks that the end was near, so the depth of my grief surprised me. I didn't try to control it.

As he slowly breathed his last, I held his hand and wept tears deep and long. I wept for the life that was no more and for the life that could have been. I wept for the blessing I never knew and for the blessing I'd discovered that I wish my father could have understood.

God doesn't want you to strive in search of blessing. He wants you to thrive in the power of His blessing.

If I were with you, I'd ask for your permission to place my hands on your shoulders, smile, look you in the eye, and say, "May God make you like Ephraim and Manasseh."

Will you join me on the pathway to blessing? I can't wait to show you how you and those you love can be transformed by the power of biblical blessing.

PART ONE

BELIEVING
the BLESSING

1

The Problem
of the Unblessed Life

On her rare visits "home," the foster child spent most of her time hiding in the closet so she wouldn't bother her mother. But sometimes she sneaked out to stare at a single frame on the wall.

"I would stand looking at this photograph and hold my breath for fear she would order me to stop looking," she said. It was a picture of the dad she'd never met. "It felt so good to have a father, to be able to look at his picture and know I belonged to him."[1]

But it was just a picture, and she never belonged to him. The little girl loved a picture in place of a real person.

"The night I met his picture I dreamed of it when I fell asleep," she said. "And I dreamed of it a thousand times afterward." During a childhood stay in the hospital for a tonsillectomy, she imagined every day that her father would suddenly, mysteriously appear. "I kept bringing my father into the hospital ward and walking him to my bed . . . and I kept bending him over my bed and having him kiss my forehead, and I gave him dialogue, too. 'You'll be well in a few days. . . . I'm very proud of the way you're behaving.'"[2]

The father, of course, never visited her and never kissed her forehead. Maybe that's why the little girl emerged from her foster homes and orphanages to spend her life acting out a role rather than being real.

Her real hair wasn't blonde.

Her real chin wasn't so angled.

Her real nose wasn't so rounded.

Her real intellect wasn't so empty.

And her real name wasn't Marilyn Monroe.

Norma Jeane Mortenson was like every child. What she wanted was a mother and father to bless her. But her mentally ill mother had no blessing to give, and her father's identity was never known. Little Norma decided to invent a father's blessing as she daydreamed in her hospital bed: *I'm very proud of the way you're behaving.* Somewhere deep in her young soul, Norma suspected something noble about her own character, but with no one to kiss her forehead and applaud her virtue, she never knew the peace and joy of a blessed life.

One Problem, Two Paths

Books have been written about Marilyn Monroe's suicidal overdose at age thirty-six, and psychotherapists have theorized about the roots of her crippling anxiety and depression.

But one thing is certain: until receiving unconditional love and affirmation, unblessed souls are bound to struggle.

Some, like the younger brother in Jesus's well-known parable of the prodigal son, run away and waste everything. Others are like the older brother in the parable who stayed at home, did all the right things that others applaud, but had no real joy in his heart.

Years ago, when our church hosted an outreach at a local homeless ministry, I met a resident named Johnny. He was wiry and his jeans hung low, not for style but for lack of a belt. He came to me for prayer.

"I'd like to find work and get my life back on track," he said.

"Why, certainly. Let's ask the Lord to grant you favor in finding a good job. What kind of work do you do?"

"I was an auto mechanic," he said. "But I've done some jail time, and now no one wants to hire me."

"Do you have family?"

"My father is still living in the area, but he doesn't want anything to do with me anymore. He wasn't the kind of father who ever told me he was proud of me or anything like that. When I was younger, I started making pretty good money as a mechanic, but my father still put me down. We were always comparing how much we made. For a little while I was making more money than him, but it didn't last long. Soon he got a raise and was winning again. That's when I got in with some wrong friends and found out how much money I could make selling drugs." Johnny hung his head in utter dejection. "I haven't even talked to my father since I got out of jail."

By withholding the blessing from Johnny, his father drove him to perform but, in so doing, poisoned his soul and sabotaged his success. It's a drama repeated a million times a day in homes, schools, athletic fields, and churches. Mothers, fathers, teachers, coaches, and preachers convince themselves, *If I tell them how proud I am, it might go to their heads. If I affirm them too much, they might not give 100 percent.*

I don't know why my own father withheld his blessing. Did he think it would puff me up? Did he think the affirmation would somehow backfire? I'll never know.

But this much is sure: when the blessing is withheld, a child's soul is tortured with the question, *Why?*

Whether you are an adored Hollywood icon, a forgotten face at the homeless shelter, or one of the millions of ordinary people who never received authentic blessing, the pain is the same.

Five Struggles of the Unblessed Life

That pain is what Jacob, the hero of our Ephraim and Manasseh story, embodied. Jacob's Hebrew name means "supplanter," or more specifically, "holder of the heel," because as he was being born, Jacob grabbed his twin brother's heel in an apparent struggle to be born first. Later, God changed his name to Israel, which means "struggles with God."

Either way, Jacob was a struggler. As we examine five of his struggles that emerged from his unblessed mentality, I encourage you to take an inventory of your own struggles.

Struggle 1: Shame

One day a man walked into a pet store and passed by a parrot that rudely squawked, "You're a loser." Every time he went near the bird, the parrot repeated the mockery: "*Squawk*. You're a loser."

Exasperated, the customer told the manager about the parrot's insults.

The frustrated store manager pulled the parrot out of its cage, shook it, and declared, "If you say it again, I'm going to wring your neck." The manager then assured the customer that the bird would no longer insult him.

After making his purchases, the customer walked by the bird on his way out and was shocked to hear it again. "*Squawk*," the parrot beckoned loudly.

"What?!" the man responded.

"You know what," the parrot replied.

Shame is an inner recording convincing us that we don't measure up. It's a nonstop, hidden squawk declaring, "You know what."

We know at least one thing about a human relationship in paradise: "The man and his wife were both naked and were not ashamed" (Gen. 2:25). The angst we feel when ashamed is often unconscious, but its gnawing pain is so uncomfortable that we'll do almost anything to avoid the feeling.

Personally, I tried to deal with shame by being whatever pleased others.

Have you ever thought, *As I am now, I can't be blessed*? That's shame's lie. And from the earliest time, that mantra haunted Jacob.

Jacob's feelings of inadequacy found root in two of the primary, timeless dispensers of shame. The first was the culture itself. He grew up in a culture that intensely favored firstborn sons. Everyone lauded the firstborn boy who would one day inherit a double portion of the estate, receive a special spoken blessing from his father, and run the family business.

By just a minute or two, Jacob was born second of the twins. *If only I'd been born before Esau,* he must have thought, *I'd be the blessed one, not him. Secondborn sons can't be fully blessed.*

What cultural voice of condemnation attacks you most? *You can't be blessed because . . .*

you aren't smart enough
you didn't come from the right family
you don't have enough money
you have made too many mistakes
you aren't pretty enough
you don't know the right people

The second source of Jacob's shame is the most common in the history of the world: an unhealthy family. One verse explains the heart of Jacob's problem: "Isaac loved Esau because he ate of his game, but Rebekah loved Jacob" (Gen. 25:28). You can imagine Isaac's parental favoritism at work: "Esau, wow, you've done it again. You're amazing with a bow and arrow." I can envision Isaac turning toward his younger son and saying, "You know, Jacob, your older brother could teach you a few things." Shame creeps in when the unblessed child wonders, *What's wrong with me? Why am I not blessed like others?*

Struggle 2: Pretense

As soon as Adam and Eve felt shame, they covered themselves.

If you and I believe that we can't be blessed as we are, we'll naturally assume that we mustn't let others see our flaws. If we grew up in a family that didn't affirm and celebrate us, it leads to a horrible, fundamental deception: *Since I'm not blessed for who I am, I need to be like someone else.*

Would you be surprised to learn that Marilyn Monroe wasn't actually the empty-headed blonde she portrayed in movies? When you read her autobiography, journals, notes, and poetry, you see a thoughtful (though darkly so), intelligent, artistic person. She yearned to be known for her acting skills rather than just her looks. She spent some of her happiest years married to an intellectual, Arthur Miller, studied art history, and accumulated a personal library of four hundred books. But no one was blessing her for those virtues. So she acted like someone else.

Like Monroe, you and I can spend a lifetime pretending.

No one was better at that than Jacob. When the time arrived for Isaac to give the much-anticipated final, special blessing to his firstborn son, Jacob conspired with his mother to trick the old, blind patriarch into thinking Jacob was actually his hairy-skinned brother. Clownishly draped in animal skins and Esau's clothes, the pretender openly lied. "Jacob said to his father, 'I am Esau your firstborn. . . . Now sit up and eat of my game, that your soul may bless me'" (Gen. 27:19).

Marilyn Monroe became an actress, literally, and Jacob acted like he was Esau because unblessed souls are rarely comfortable in their own skin.

Do you ever feel like you need to be like someone else in order to be blessed? If someone affirms your persona, they haven't affirmed you. That's why pretense begets loneliness.

Struggle 3: Loneliness

In the posthumous publication of Marilyn Monroe's journals, an early entry begins, "Alone!!!!!! I am alone I am always alone no matter what." Her cursive script, one observer noted, "leans dangerously forward, as if about to fall off a cliff."[3] Ironically, the more she sought adoration, the lonelier she became.

Upon learning that Esau wanted to murder his thieving brother, Rebekah urged her favored son to flee for his life (Gen. 27:43–45). Jacob had hoped his desperate trick for attention would encircle him with love; instead, it made him a lonely fugitive.

Loneliness has become epidemic in America. A CBS News feature asserted some years ago, "The American Sociological Review may have just published the social health equivalent of the 1964 Surgeon General's report that declared smoking causes cancer."[4] Researchers at Duke and the University of Arizona discovered that "the number of people saying there is no one with whom they discuss important matters nearly tripled."[5] Other research has revealed similar alarming trends. Forty percent of Americans don't feel like their relationships are meaningful, and twenty percent declare themselves lonely or socially isolated.[6] A plethora of causes have been proposed, such as the surge of social media, the depersonalization of the workplace, and the aging of America. But little attention has been given to what may be the greatest root of American loneliness—the absence of blessing, which creates shame, isolation, and pretense.

At the end of each day of creation, the Lord celebrated His handiwork: "God saw that it was good" (Gen. 1:10). But amid the glory of creation, one thing wasn't good in paradise. "Then the LORD God said, 'It is not good that the man should be alone'" (2:18). Adam was perfect but incomplete. With the biblical creation account in mind, it's not surprising that recent science has found conclusive links between loneliness and a variety of illnesses like heart disease and dementia.

Loneliness hurts—literally.[7] God has designed you for relationship. But all intimacy depends on authenticity. When you are blessed like Ephraim and Manasseh, you can be healed of the shame that tempts you to hide your real self, and in that wholeness, you can discover the joy of real relationships.

Struggle 4: Drift

In the early eighties, a psychoanalyst observed that, like the beloved character in J. M. Barrie's play, some men never seem to grow up. He dubbed the problem "The Peter Pan Syndrome."[8] Though not a clinically recognized diagnosis, the syndrome refers to something we all have seen—a bright, gifted young adult who struggles to accept responsibility and become focused.

After he pretended to be his brother in order to steal Esau's blessing, Jacob fled for his life, lost all focus, and wandered for years. His life was being shaped by what he was avoiding. Instead of joyfully embracing adult responsibilities, he kept pursuing a fanciful vision of the blessed life. Instead of moving toward an authentic, mature goal, he drifted without purpose.

In the happiest part of my childhood, I spent hours in the surf of Myrtle Beach, jumping breakers, catching waves on the raft, and just goofing off in the warm Atlantic with my brothers and friends. More than once, enjoying the fun, I'd look ashore and find myself lost because I'd drifted hundreds of yards down the beach. Similarly, if we don't pay attention, the unseen current of life can carry us far from our God-given destiny.

Unblessed lives are rarely focused. Bestselling author Michael Hyatt identifies confusion as the first consequence of drifting. "There's no larger story to provide meaning to life's smaller dramas. . . . We eventually wonder if our life has any meaning and despair of finding purpose."[9]

I remember being surprised when a middle-aged parishioner reflected on the worst day of his life. It wasn't a day a loved one had died or a day a doctor had diagnosed a horrid disease. Instead, it was a day in his young adulthood when he asked his father a simple question.

"Dad, what do you think I should do with my life?"

"I don't know, Son. That's something you have to figure out for yourself," his father replied abruptly.

That was the worst day of his life?

"Wow," I said to the man. "What hurt so much about your father's response?"

"When my dad had no counsel for my life direction, it seemed he had no recognition of my gifts—no belief in my value. He might as well have said, 'Son, you don't have anything to offer this world.'"

This man didn't need or want his father to dictate a direction for him, but he desperately needed his father's affirmation and faith so he could flourish.

Without authentic blessing, we, like Jacob, can look back and discover we've spent years drifting.

Struggle 5: Relationship Problems

Jacob was close with his mother but distant from his dad. His twin brother hated him. But the real trouble started when he fell in love at first sight with Rachel.

Why such emotion upon his first sight of her? Perhaps Jacob wept at the mere possibility of love. The struggler hastily vowed to Laban, "I will serve you seven years for your younger daughter Rachel" (Gen. 29:18). Of course, when you love someone, you naturally make sacrifices, but Jacob had it backwards. Jacob's problem was that he, like most who have missed the blessing, thought he had to prove his value before he could experience love.

And his relationship troubles had only begun. Recognizing that Jacob would work for love, Laban tricked the trickster. He somehow subbed in his older daughter, Leah, on Jacob's wedding night, and Jacob married the wrong woman. He pledged another seven years of labor for Rachel.

If you and I don't feel blessed, there's no end to how hard we'll work to try to attain the blessing we crave. If we aren't securely blessed, we'll find it hard to be at peace with those we love because their imperfections will threaten our sense of worth.

Like with the picture of her father that Marilyn Monroe saw on the wall, Jacob set his affection upon the image of Rachel but had little capacity to learn and grow and thrive in the beautiful, messy covenant of marriage. Soon, Rachel and Leah were bringing their maidservants Bilhah and Zilpah into a competition to bear more children for Jacob.

"I Will Not Let You Go Unless You Bless Me"

Amid all his misguided struggles, one instinct was on target: Jacob knew he needed to be blessed. He tried to buy the blessing. He tried to steal the blessing. He tried to work for the blessing. And then he wrestled for it.

In fearful anticipation of a reunion with his brother, Jacob sent his family, servants, and possessions across the Jabbok River toward home. "Jacob was left alone. And a man wrestled with him until the breaking of the day" (Gen. 32:24). The all-night struggle culminated when the messenger of God dislocated Jacob's hip. Jacob, though disabled, would not yield. When dawn broke, the angelic wrestler commanded Jacob to let him go. "But Jacob said, 'I will not let you go unless you bless me'" (Gen. 32:26).

Jacob didn't know the right way to receive the blessing, but he knew his life would never be fulfilled without it.

I will not let you go unless you bless me.

Have you ever fought for a blessing like that?

Not long after my dad shared that index card of blessing with me in the counselor's office, his brilliant mind was lost to dementia and he was relegated to skilled care. One sunny day I was pushing his wheelchair into the open-air courtyard so he could feel the warmth and hear the rustle of the leaves. Our ministry had just launched a radio program, and remembering how my father had started his career on the radio, I said, "Dad, we've just started airing our new radio program on five stations in several different states."

In a rare, lucid moment, Dad lifted his head, smiled, and said, "Well, that's great."

I loved his smile, but I wished for more. I longed for my eloquent broadcaster father to rise from his wheelchair, lay his hands on my head, and prophetically announce, "Alan, you are my son in whom I'm pleased. Whatever gift of communication started in me now abides in you, but for a greater purpose. May God make you like Ephraim and Manasseh, more fulfilled and fruitful than you've ever imagined. You have a special gift, my son, and I envision you helping hundreds of thousands of people." But his body had no strength to rise from the wheelchair, and his spirit had no capacity to arise and affirm my destiny.

Like Jacob, I knew I'd never be okay unless I was blessed.

If you've longed for blessing, it's worth wrestling for. It's worth learning all you can about how to receive blessing from God, from others, and from your own redeemed self-talk. That's been my journey, and it can be yours too.

After Johnny shared his pain with me that day at the mission, I explained to him the power of blessing, and he said he wanted it. We took hands and looked eye to eye, and I said, "Johnny, you are a child of God, created in His image, and you have a wonderful purpose in this world. You have a mechanical mind, and you are good with your hands. I bless that good mind and those good hands, and I believe

God has the right job for you." As I continued, Johnny's weathered face softened and tears rolled down it. I never saw him again, but I believe the power of blessing began shaping his life that day.

Marilyn Monroe had no one to bless her.

"I longed for a miracle," Arthur Miller wrote. "[But] I had no saving mystery to offer her; nor could her hand be taken if she would not hold it out. I had lost my faith in a lasting cure . . . and wondered if indeed it would come from any human agency at all."[10]

What if Miller had known how to bless her?

What if you and I knew how to bless our own lives and the lives of those we love?

Unblessed, Marilyn chronically struggled with depression, once writing: "Help help Help I feel life coming closer when all I want Is to die."[11]

The toxicology report stated the cause of her death by suicide as "acute barbiturate poisoning." But the death certificate aptly could have read "starved for blessing."

2

Why Blessing Precedes Success

"On my first day in the seventh grade, I discovered I was poor."

Those are the words of one of the smartest men I know, a longtime friend and colleague of mine, Mickey Thigpen—a thin, sixty-something, eclectic, baseball-loving former hippie who really likes serving Jesus. His parents had only six years of formal education each. His dad worked in the dust of the sawmill in Kinston, North Carolina, for decades until it closed. His mother worked second shift in the weaving line in the Kinston cotton mill for over forty years.

Like a lot of us, Mickey said, "Every good thing in my story begins with a praying mother."

Mickey never thought much about his low-income upbringing in East Kinston until he went to junior high at

Harvey School. It was on the other side of town—Mickey's people called it the rich side. Because the new school was farther away, Mickey's folks had to drive him each morning, but he felt so embarrassed by his parents' old car that he asked to be dropped off down the street. Sometimes he took a farther detour, walking blocks out of his way, so he wouldn't be seen approaching school from the poor side of town.

Mickey demonstrated scholastic aptitude at Harvey, but even that made him lonely. "None of my friends from East Kinston were in the advanced sections, so I never saw them. I was manifestly poor and manifestly different."

But there were bright spots amid the darkness of those junior high years. One light stands out in particular—Mrs. Betsy Harper. She taught North Carolina history and, for some reason, made Mickey her assistant in eighth grade.

When Mickey moved up to Grainger High for his freshman year, it so happened that Mrs. Harper relocated as well. Her room was across from Mrs. Piaski's, where Mickey took first-year Latin. Early in the fall of ninth grade, the bell rang and Mickey emerged from Mrs. Piaski's class with a test paper in his hand. He'd gotten a C on the Latin quiz. Mrs. Harper was standing outside her room and, as Mickey was walking by, asked to see the paper he was carrying.

"This is the last C you'll ever get," Mrs. Harper said confidently, "because you're going to be a Morehead Scholar."

Mickey didn't know what a Morehead Scholar was, so he looked it up. Modeled after the Rhodes scholarship, the Morehead (now the Morehead-Cain) was the first merit scholarship program established in the United States. It is the most competitive, prestigious scholarship in the university system of North Carolina. The scholars receive not only full tuition, room, board, a computer, and three enriching summer experiences but also the enduring prestige of being a Morehead Scholar.

When you consider Mickey's background, Mrs. Harper's prophetic blessing seemed preposterous. But it wasn't to the ninth grader.

"I believed her completely," Mickey said, "and took her words to be my future."

Three years later, against all odds, Mickey Thigpen was awarded the Morehead Scholarship.

He went on to do what I think John Motley Morehead III had dreamed of when founding the scholarship. Mickey invested himself into others' lives. For decades, he served marginalized people in our state by developing and operating group homes for the disabled.

His remarkable story prompts the question, Would Mickey have become a Morehead Scholar if Mrs. Harper hadn't blessed him that day?

Be assured, I believe God is sovereign. If God wanted Mickey Thigpen to have a Morehead Scholarship, He most certainly could have brought that about with or without Mrs. Harper. But would He have?

I'm convinced God has so ordained the practice of blessing that our future fruitfulness depends on it.

Blessed, *Then* Success

Most people think the Christian message declares, "Follow Christ. Serve. Study. Pray. Give. And God will bless you."

But that's not the message of the Bible. In fact, that is precisely what the Christian gospel *isn't*. The true gospel declares that in Christ, God has blessed you beyond measure. Therefore, follow Him, serve, study, pray, and give with joy.

Genesis 1:28 is one of the most important verses in the Bible. Note well the order of events: "God blessed them. And God said to them, 'Be fruitful and multiply and fill the earth and subdue it, and have dominion.'"

God blessed Adam and Eve and *then* released them to be fruitful, multiply, and rule. For most of my life, I believed the opposite. I assumed that if I performed well (bore fruit), worked hard (multiplied), and succeeded (ruled), *then* I would be blessed. But Genesis 1:28 radically upends the order of events. With God, the blessing is not the reward for productivity—it's the power for it.

God designed blessing as the fuel for the fruitfulness of our lives. It's wonderful news because, if the blessing comes first, then our current circumstances and past failures don't limit our future. It means we should start blessing others now even if they haven't done anything to warrant our affirmation.

In the early nineties, a poster of Olympic Gold medalist alpine skier Tommy Moe hung on the wall of the ski center in Squaw Valley, California, where a little girl named Julia hung out. When she was nine, Julia sketched her own poster using a black marker. She drew herself racing down the mountain like Moe, the Hall of Famer, and at the bottom of her self-made poster, the third grader inscribed "4-Time Olympic gold medalist—Julia Mancuso."[1]

At the 2006 Turin Winter Olympics, little Julia's prophetic poster came true. Her gold medal in the giant slalom shocked the skiing world because she'd not had a particularly successful season. But Julia had seen it coming ever since the day she blessed her own life with a marker and a poster. She won four medals in three different Olympics—the most ever for a female American alpine skier.[2]

As with Mickey, I wonder, if Julia hadn't drawn that picture, would she have won the gold?

Just because a little girl announces herself as an Olympic medalist doesn't magically assure her of the gold. I announced myself as Superman when I was nine, but I never flew.

On the other hand, has there ever been a person on the Olympic platform who didn't draw a mental picture of themselves being there?

God Doesn't Test and Then Bless

My whole life I was taught, *Do well on the test and then you'll be blessed.*

So in an effort to be blessed, I'd study hard for tests. I had more than one teacher tell me that the test is actually a learning opportunity—a chance to show how much you know. I never saw it that way. It was hard to believe that the blessing could come first.

Work hard, prove yourself, and maybe you'll be blessed with a promotion. Develop a good personality, take care of your looks, and maybe you'll be blessed with a good relationship. Make a lot of money, be generous, and maybe people will like you a lot. That seems to be the way the world works.

Though any Christian communicator should believe in grace, most preachers communicate a mixed message.

I think of a moving sermon illustration about trust that features a little girl whose father gave her an artificial pearl necklace. The girl adored the faux pearls, wearing them all the time and keeping them under her pillow at night. After years of cherishing the necklace, she was mystified when one night her father said, "Sweetheart, will you give me your pearls?"

"But, Daddy," she replied, "I love these pearls. They are my favorite thing in the whole wide world."

"Sweetheart, do you trust me?"

"Yes, Daddy."

"If you trust me, will you give me your pearls?"

Fighting back tears, the little girl reached under her pillow, pulled out the string of pearls, and handed them slowly to her father.

"Now I have something for you," he said with a smile.

He pulled a package from behind his back and gave it to his daughter. She opened the box, and there, glistening before her eyes, was a set of real pearls.

"These pearls are real, sweetheart. They're yours now. I'm glad you trusted me enough to make the trade."

This has all the makings of a beautiful sermon illustration. The childlike trust. The father's love. The letting go. The generous heart of God. But the beautiful story has a gaping theological flaw. God doesn't test us before He blesses us. Paul preached just the opposite: "For while we were still weak, at the right time Christ died for the ungodly. . . . God shows his love for us in that while we were still sinners, Christ died for us" (Rom. 5:6, 8).

If God had required us to let go of all our counterfeit treasures before giving us the real treasure of Christ, Jesus would have never come. God blesses us in order to make us faithful, not because we've proven ourselves faithful already.

Trying hard to deserve God's blessing is what Paul means when he talks about living under the law. That sort of moralistic living doesn't lead to blessing but instead invokes the opposite: "For all who rely on works of the law are under a curse; for it is written, 'Cursed be everyone who does not abide by all things written in the Book of the Law, and do them'" (Gal. 3:10). Ironically, the harder you try to *prove* yourself worthy of being blessed, the less you can actually *be* blessed because the blessing of God is a gift.

I think that's why Israel's most important family blessing highlights two people who have no known accomplishments to their names. We don't know whether Ephraim and Manasseh were obedient kids or rebels. We have no assurance that they kept the Torah, honored their parents, or stayed pure in the midst of secular Egypt. We aren't told those things because if we were, we'd assume those are the reasons we use their names in the blessing. When Jacob blessed Ephraim and Manasseh, it wasn't because he'd tested them and found them worthy. It was because he finally understood that blessing, like all grace, must be given without conditions.

To be true to the gospel, the above sermon illustration needs a different sequence. Imagine it this way: instead of hiding the pearls to test his daughter's trust, the father smiles, kneels by his little girl's bed, and hands her a bright package. Then, after she's opened it and seen the shimmering real pearls, he says, "Sweetheart, would you like to trade in your old, pretend pearls for these real ones?" The little girl quickly surrenders the phony for the authentic because her father's blessing has empowered her obedience.

Why the Blessing Must Come First

Though many of us grew up thinking, *First I succeed and then I'm blessed*, the gospel reverses the order—*I can succeed because I'm blessed.* Under the power of blessing, we don't work hard in order to have hope—we work hard *because* we have hope. As blessed people, we don't excel in order to prove who we are—we excel because we know who we are.

1) Hope Comes before Hard Work

Without blessing, there's no hope. And without hope, there's no chance of victory. If you're a football fan, you've seen it happen. Your team is in a close game in the fourth quarter, when all of a sudden, the opponent intercepts a pass and scampers into the end zone. You can almost literally see your team deflate. The lead suddenly feels insurmountable. After the kickoff, the offense returns to the field to go through the motions, but they've clearly given up.

When you think you can't win, it's almost impossible to make yourself try. If you want the energy, passion, and commitment that lead to success, hope must come first.

In 2009, a University of Minnesota study of twenty thousand teenagers revealed that nearly 15 percent of all teens believe they are going to die young. The sad revelation challenges the conventional hypothesis about adolescent irresponsibility. We've presumed that if a seventeen-year-old drives ninety miles per hour, experiments with drugs, or walks near the edge of a cliff, it's because he feels invincible, immortal. But after the study, lead researcher Dr. Iris Borowsky postulated that many teens act foolishly because they feel hopeless and figure that not much is at stake.[3]

The modern English usage of the word *hope* is quite different from the concept in the Bible. If you ask a little girl what she wants for Christmas and she replies, "I hope I get a pony," she doesn't mean that she actually believes she will get a pony. She means that she wishes she'd get a pony but that, in reality, it's quite unlikely. Similarly, buying a lottery ticket in the "hope" of winning one hundred million dollars is just wishful thinking.

The Bible's definition of hope is entirely different.

When Jeremiah prophesied, "For I know the plans I have for you . . . to give you a future and a hope" (Jer. 29:11), the Lord didn't want the Babylonian exiles to start wishing for a long shot. He wanted them to know for sure that He would bring them home. When Peter wrote about the "living hope . . . kept in heaven for you" (1 Pet. 1:3–4), he wasn't speaking of eternal glory like a little girl wishing for a pony at Christmas. In the Bible, hope is the blissful certainty of future blessedness that empowers you today.

If you were to ask an excited little girl in December why she's so happy, she'd say, "Because Christmas is coming!" That's hope. She is certain that December 25 is coming. Because of the hope of Christmas, the whole family has been putting out decorations, adorning the tree, and wrapping presents. Hope isn't wishful thinking. It's joyful expectancy powerful enough to rearrange your whole life.

Before Mrs. Harper blessed Mickey, he had no hope of winning the Morehead Scholarship. The hope of the scholarship turned Mickey into a scholar. Beforehand, he was brilliant but content to get a C. Yet once hope emerged in his heart, without conscious thought, Mickey was energized as a student. He didn't win the Morehead Scholarship just because a teacher announced it. He won it because he aligned his studies and extracurricular pursuits toward it.

After Julia Mancuso drew a picture of herself winning the Olympic gold, did she go sit on the couch and eat potato chips while waiting on someone to put the medal around her neck? No, she hit the slopes every day, practicing with all her might.

Blessing gives birth to hope, which then gives birth to the energy, passion, and commitment that will bring success.

2) Positive Identity Comes before Productivity

In 1964, the principal of Spruce Elementary School in San Francisco announced to the teachers that she'd given permission for Harvard psychologist Robert Rosenthal to administer a new sort of IQ test to the students. Later, the teachers were informed that the new testing tool had identified some students who were poised to bloom academically. The next year, as predicted, the students identified as likely to excel bloomed marvelously. These special first graders increased their IQ scores by a dramatic twenty-seven points. Only afterward did the researcher reveal the truth to the teachers. The alleged newfangled intelligence test was actually just the standard IQ test, and the bloomers were not actually smarter—they were chosen at random. Average students whom teachers erroneously believed to be above average were significantly more likely to excel.

Though Rosenthal's research was challenged vigorously, dozens of studies have since confirmed the concept. When managers have positive thoughts about employees' potential, the workers do better work. When military instructors believe they have higher-level recruits, the soldiers perform better. Even couples who have been told they are a good match interact more positively with one another.[4]

If students, workers, soldiers, and spouses thrive just because someone believes positive things about them, how much more powerful is biblical, faith-filled blessing when spoken directly into our hearts?

Mrs. Harper's words to Mickey became powerful because he took on a new identity. "I believed her completely and took her words to be my future," he said. In a real sense, Mickey became a Morehead Scholar the day that Mrs. Harper told him he was one. As a nine-year-old, Julia Mancuso took on the identity of an Olympian.

We don't choose how to live and then form an identity to match it. We form an identity and then live to match it.

If you'd like to perform better on an upcoming test, it'll help if you spend a few minutes envisioning yourself as smart. At least that's what one Dutch research study proved. Researchers gave a group of random students forty-two challenging questions taken from the well-known board game Trivial Pursuit. According to their instructions, half the participants spent five minutes before the quiz writing down what they thought it would be like to be a professor. The other half were told to spend five minutes writing down what it might be like to be a rude, violent sports fan. Those who imagined being a professor got 55.6 percent of the questions correct, whereas the "hooligan" group answered only 42.6 percent correctly.[5]

If you become smarter by spending five minutes imagining yourself as a scholar, what might happen if you spent time every day meditating on the psalmist's assurance that

God made you "a little lower than the angels" (Ps. 8:5 NIV) or on Paul's exclamation that you've been given "the mind of Christ" (1 Cor. 2:16)?

How we think about ourselves determines how we live. That's why names are so important. What others call us, and what we call ourselves, shapes the direction of our lives. We often don't pay attention to the meaning of names in Western culture, but not so in the ancient Middle East. Everyone knew the meaning of names. Later, we'll discover deep meaning in the names of Ephraim and Manasseh, but first, consider Jacob, whose name was changed to Israel—an identity so important that a whole nation bears the title.

As we've seen, after Jacob duped his father in order to steal Esau's blessing, he ran away for fear of Esau's revenge. After years of loneliness, drift, and marriage struggles, Jacob finally planned to meet Esau again. But before that, he wrestled a heavenly being all night long. Remember how he wouldn't let go until the angel blessed him? The heavenly wrestler responded by changing the patriarch's name: "Your name shall no longer be called Jacob, but Israel, for you have striven with God and with men, and have prevailed" (Gen. 32:28).

Perhaps the greatest blessing we can ever receive is to hear who we truly are. Before Jacob could bless Ephraim and Manasseh, he needed to discover his own true identity. So God sent a messenger to bless the struggler.

Jacob means "one who grasps the heel." In that sense, it means "struggles with people." His new name, Israel, means, "struggles with God." How could it be a blessing to have his name changed from "struggles with people" to "struggles with God"? Jacob, like all of us, would face troubles in this world, but as Israel, he would learn to bring his heartaches to God instead of trying to work them out by his own cleverness. Though Jacob had spent most of his life trying to prove himself to others, God wanted him to know his real identity: Israel, a blessed man who had nothing to prove—a man who, instead of deceiving and cheating others, brought his struggles to God.

The Day This Book Was Born

When I began to understand the power of blessing, I started changing my self-talk, but I also instinctively sought other spiritual friends who could speak godly vision into my life. God gave me a mentor in a spiritual mountain of a man named Dudley Hall. He is an accomplished author, Bible teacher, and leader. He let me spend time with him. And after a while, it became clear that he was my spiritual father.

Many years ago, Dudley invited me to come speak at his national conference, and when he introduced me to the crowd, he said, "I think Alan is one of the finest communicators of the gospel in the nation." It would have been enough for him to whisper those words to me privately, but when he blessed me publicly like that, a mysterious, healing virtue flowed into me.

The affirmation I had so longed to hear from my dad finally came from a different communicator. As Dudley's words drifted over the crowd, I stepped onto the stage not puffed up but empowered. A spiritual mentor's blessing will empower our deepest, God-given dreams.

Some years later, Dudley's son, David, was married in my home church. I assisted with the wedding, enjoyed the reception afterward, and got home late that Saturday night. I pulled out the sermon I'd planned to preach the next day. It was far from my best. I'd been busy, my study was incomplete, and it contained no powerful revelation. I was preaching on a new, unfamiliar text from Genesis 48 about the strange blessing of two obscure grandsons.

Around midnight, a thought occurred to me. *Dudley will be on the second pew tomorrow morning. My spiritual father thinks I'm an excellent communicator of the gospel, and the flimsy preparation I've given this message won't do.* So I said good night to my wife, Anne, put my nose back in the Bible, and said, "Lord, show me something more in this text."

I stayed up half that night not because I was afraid of failing but because my spiritual father had blessed my preaching. I didn't rewrite that sermon to make Dudley proud. I rewrote it because he was already proud.

On that Sunday morning in the fall of 2007, I preached on the blessing of Ephraim and Manasseh. As I crossed my arms like Jacob, I caught Dudley's eyes—misted over like mine.

Though I didn't know it at the time, that was the day this book was born.

3

If You Can See It, You Can Be It

Reformed theologian John Calvin said the Scriptures are like spectacles for the aged.[1] Without the lens of divine revelation, everything we see, including ourselves, is blurred by our own sin.

I wasn't aged when I discovered I needed glasses. My fourth grade teacher noticed me squinting at the chalkboard. I remember the ride home from the optician, and I was amazed that I could see individual leaves on trees. I didn't know trees looked like that—dappled and dancing around. I had always thought they were green blobs.

The problem with nearsightedness is that you don't know what you're not seeing, and no amount of trying harder to see better makes anything clearer. That's why telling people to work harder at being good is like telling people with blurred vision to squint harder.

Religion shames people when they can't read the chalk-board. Blessing gives them new lenses.

The principle of blessing makes your job as a parent, spouse, friend, teacher, employer, or coach simple: just show people who they were made to be.

The Ephraim and Manasseh blessing, like all blessing, isn't about reciting the words as much as it is about giving people new lenses so they see themselves as God sees them. In part 2, we'll see up close why God wants you to be like Ephraim and Manasseh. This blessing will become your spiritual lens to help you see yourself in Christ: totally accepted, free of shame, fashioned for fruitfulness, and undeservedly favored.

The Ephraim and Manasseh blessing, like all blessing, isn't a picture of what you aren't and should try harder to become. It's a picture of who you already are.

The Immortal Tadpole

Does God sometimes put odd things in our lives to teach us important lessons? I guess if He gave Hosea a prostitute wife and sent a worm to eat Jonah's shade plant, He could give me an immortal tadpole.

The never-changing tadpole actually belonged to my daughter, Abby. When she was five, she came home from her preschool with it. It seemed simple enough—the tadpole was destined to become a frog in front of our eyes. Of course, we needed to dechlorinate the water and change it often. And, as it turns out, tadpoles are picky eaters. We had to boil spinach, freeze it in ziplock bags, and sprinkle small portions into the tadpole bowl each day. But no worries—in a matter of a few weeks, our spinach-boiling and water-changing duties would be over and we would have a full-fledged frog that we could release into the wild.

Abby placed her tadpole's jar on a shelf in her room, and we began feeding it spinach. The tadpole grew nicely over the next few days. After two weeks, the other preschoolers' tadpoles had started sprouting legs and dropping tails. But Abby's didn't. Her tadpole kept swimming around its bowl and eating frozen spinach. Then two months went by.

Anne bumped into Abby's preschool teacher, Miss Nikki, at the ten-week mark. "Hey, Nikki, when in the world is the tadpole going to turn into a frog?"

"What are you talking about?" Miss Nikki asked.

"The tadpole you sent home with Abby. When will it grow legs and all that?"

"Uh, that should have happened long ago. Are you saying your tadpole is still a tadpole?"

"Yep—totally tadpole. Zero frog."

"That's impossible."

Another impossible month went by. And another. And another. A year and a half later, Abby's tadpole was still a tadpole. After consulting erudite scientific sites like Wikipedia and allaboutfrogs.org, I discovered that Miss Nikki was right—it *is* impossible for a tadpole to still be a tadpole after eighteen months. We were the only family in the history of the world to own an immortal, unchangeable pet tadpole.

One day an older Abby came home from summer camp with an aquatic frog. We were suddenly proud owners of both a tadpole and a frog. We considered placing them in the same bowl, but we were concerned that the unusually large immortal tadpole would eat the smaller though fully developed frog. So we put the aquatic frog in its own bowl next to the tadpole on the shelf in Abby's room.

The next day, my seven-year-old daughter called me at the office. "Daddy, Daddy, you won't believe it!"

"What!"

"My tadpole has grown legs!"

"What? Are you serious? Are you sure you aren't just looking at your new frog?"

"Daddy, I'm telling you the truth. My tadpole has legs!"

Since it's part of my job to bear witness to miracles, I packed up and dashed home. Not only did the tadpole have legs, but it also had started losing its tail. By the next day, a full metamorphosis had taken place. Within forty-eight hours of placing a real frog next to its bowl, the immortal tadpole had transformed into a full frog.

Evidently, it just needed to see what it really was.

I think that's how you and I change—not by trying harder to become something better but by being blessed with a vision of who we are designed to be. I bet you can think of someone you love who is gifted but who is underachieving because they don't believe it. You might know a girl who is lovely and smart, but because she doesn't feel that way about herself, she keeps dating guys who are the opposite. Perhaps you love someone who is discouraged and depressed because he feels like a failure.

Underachievers don't start excelling because someone tells them to try harder. Girls don't pick the right guys because we tell them they ought to be pure. Depressed people don't get better because we tell them to be happy. People don't change until they see themselves differently.

If you feel like a tadpole today, you don't need to try harder to grow legs—you just need a new vision of your life. Your metamorphosis will come when you see what God has designed you to be.

The East Lake Miracle

There was a time when the East Lake area of Atlanta was gorgeous—anchored by the historic Bobby Jones golf course. But by the 1960s, the former getaway for Atlanta's affluent citizenry had fallen into utter disrepair, and in 1970, a public housing project was erected on East Lake's former No. 2 golf course.

The East Lake Meadows public housing development never was good, but by 1995, it was awful. Drugs and gangs had taken over, and the crime rate was eighteen times the national average. Conditions in the neighborhood grew so bad that local police dubbed it "Little Vietnam."

When Anne and I lived in Atlanta in the 1980s, Anne volunteered at the women's shelter and I worked at a downtown church, but honestly, I wouldn't have dared spend time in East Lake. Trash covered the streets. Bullet holes dotted windows and doorways. Thugs traded drugs in broad daylight. The employment rate (employment, not unemployment) was 14 percent. It was one of the worst neighborhoods in the country, and everyone had given up on it.

Except one man. Tom Cousins, a humble real estate developer, had brought professional sports to Atlanta, built its biggest skyscraper, and quietly given away millions. But when he saw the East Lake neighborhood, he couldn't believe such a thing could exist in America and decided to do something about it. When he discovered that the famous East Lake golf course was in disrepair and on the edge of bankruptcy, he decided to buy it and use it as a catalyst for change in the neighborhood. He invited one hundred businessmen to join the club for $200,000 each and pledged to use the $20 million to revive the crime-ridden housing project across the street.

They tore down the decrepit apartments and replaced them with attractive new buildings that were occupied half by publicly assisted residents and half by full-paying, middle-income families. I saw an interview in which Cousins said something like, "I realized if I had grown up in that neighborhood, I probably would be uneducated, selling drugs, and in jail. So I just wanted to see what would happen if underprivileged children had the opportunity to see what normal, happy, hardworking families look like. I just wanted a disadvantaged child to have the chance to see a father get the newspaper from the driveway with his cup of coffee, go to work, and come back home in the evening to help his kids with their homework."

What would happen if children saw what they could be?

The results were astonishing. In 1995, only 5 percent of fifth graders in East Lake met state math standards. Within ten years, after a new charter school was developed, 78 percent did. The crime rate dropped 95 percent. The percentage of welfare recipients decreased from 58 to 5. The employment rate for people on public assistance rose from 14 percent to 71 percent. With partnership from Warren Buffett, Cousins has seen the same kind of effect in other communities around the nation.[2]

Get Your Tadpoles around Some Frogs

Anne and I rooted our whole parenting adventure in the principle of blessing because we didn't want to spend our energy managing behavior as much as we wanted to shape identity. Blessing is more than occasional, verbal affirmation. Blessing is a consistent commitment to help others gain godly vision of their lives.

It's better to help a kid see himself as a good student than it is to nag him about studying harder. If a kid sees herself as an A student, she'll do what it takes to make A's. When our kids acted foolishly, we didn't call them stupid; we called them smart. Anne had a great line: "God gave you a great brain, so I expect you to use it." We also didn't let them watch worthless shows that depicted kids acting like brats. I never wanted them to get the idea that kids are ungrateful whiners. We watched over their friendships carefully. They didn't know it, but we more or less picked their peers for them.

You know who is helping your kids' self-image and who isn't. If you want your tadpoles to become hoppers, you need to show them some well-developed frogs.

Jeff Deaton's parents knew they had a fine tadpole of a son, so they let him spend a lot of time around some fine frogs. Jeff's a reproductive endocrinologist, which means he's a fertility doctor. So whenever I introduce him I say, "Meet Jeff. He's gotten a lot of women pregnant in our city." I mean it as a blessing.

Jeff wasn't a likely candidate to become one of the nation's pioneers in fertility medicine. In fact, it's a little surprising he went to college, much less got a full ride to Vanderbilt. Most folks in his hometown planned on working a local job after high school. In his early years, Jeff couldn't have seen himself excelling in medical school, residency, and fellowship training. He grew up the youngest of three in a small Tennessee town. When he was a little boy, his brother, who was eight years older, would take him to Buddies Place, where they'd walk up three flights of creaky stairs to the pool hall and bar. The elder brother would sit ten-year-old Jeff on a bar stool while he hustled pool. Jeff didn't mind because the bartender would usually pull out a frosted mug of chocolate milk for the bar's youngest patron.

His parents were wonderful, loving people who, in Jeff's words, "couldn't see a different future for me. They didn't have the words to encourage a life they could not envision." When Dr. and Mrs. Harrison showed interest in him, Jeff's parents were happy for it. His mom worked for Dr. Harrison's pediatric office, but Jeff's real inroad with the Harrisons was their daughter. Since Jeff was a champion mathematician, the Harrisons asked him to tutor their high school daughter in math. So throughout high school, Jeff spent a couple nights a week at the esteemed doctor's house, tutoring one of the cutest, most popular girls in town. Not a bad gig, but as interested as Jeff was in the girl, he was even more interested in the doctor and his wife.

"They spoke of subjects that were different from what I heard in my house," Jeff said. "I learned of a whole other world, one that seemed so expansive. I watched an older couple push themselves to learn. Before the Harrisons, I assumed that all learning stopped after high school or college."

Day after day, the Harrisons showed Jeff how much they believed in him, affirming not only his math intellect but also the whole potential of his life.

When Jeff graduated from med school, Mrs. Harrison wrote a letter to the editor of the local paper saying how proud their little community should be. I wonder how she would feel if she met a new mom and dad who wouldn't have a baby today if the Harrisons hadn't blessed Jeff Deaton.

When someone blesses you, they don't make you valuable; they just help you see the value you haven't known. If a petroleum geologist informed you that you had a lucrative oil reserve in your backyard, he wouldn't make you wealthy; he'd simply point out the wealth you hadn't seen. The frog is already in the tadpole—it just needs to be called forth.

Choosing Frog over Tadpole

I love the trick my cute Anne sometimes uses in her opening talk at a women's conference. She'll turn toward the left side of the room and say, "Ladies, you need to be better women. You need to be better wives. You have to respect your husbands more, and you must quit nagging so much. You ought to be better mothers too. You need to be more patient and less lazy and do a better job of training up your children. You need to read your Bible more, pray more, exercise more, and give more." The women's shoulders sag, they nod slowly, and you can just feel the joy being sucked out of the room.

Then Anne turns to the right side of the room, smiles, and declares, "Ladies, you are the daughters of the Most High God! As His beloved ones, not only have you been assured of eternal glory, but you have already been seated with Christ in the heavenlies. You're more than conquerors. Ladies, I believe you can do all things through Christ who gives you strength. You're the light of the world, and you're destined to make a difference." You can feel the power and joy of the Holy Spirit flowing as you see the ladies' faces turn radiant.

Then Anne asks all the women, "Which side of the room do you want to be on?"

It's not that the things she said to the ladies on the left were wrong. In fact, it was all likely true. Probably all the women should be better wives, mothers, and followers of Christ. They likely all could use some more patience and surely could practice spiritual disciplines more regularly. It's not that the moralistic exhortations weren't true; they just weren't helpful.

When we spend time telling young frogs how much they still look like tadpoles, they're likely to stay tadpoles longer. Everyone you meet is, in a sense, both a tadpole and a frog. The best way to grow as a Christian is to quit listening to your own deceived heart and start listening deeply to what God has to say about who you are:

When you sin, God calls you "holy" (Heb. 10:10 NIV).

When you feel bland, God calls you the "salt of the earth" (Matt. 5:13).

When your money runs out, God calls you "rich in every way" (1 Cor. 1:5 NCV).

When your memory slips, God says you have the "mind of Christ" (1 Cor. 2:16).

When you feel ashamed, God calls you "blameless" (Eph. 1:4).

When you've done nothing majestic, God calls you a "royal priesthood" (1 Pet. 2:9).

In one sense, the whole biblical narrative revolves around the question, Will God's people believe God's vision for their lives, or will they live according to their own blurred perspective?

Would Adam and Eve believe God's vision for their lives as His beloved, fruitful children, or would they listen to the serpent who told them they weren't fully blessed because they hadn't tasted of the tree in the middle of the garden? Would Abraham believe himself to be the father of a nation though he was old and childless? Would Moses believe himself to be a deliverer though Pharaoh had all the power? When Moses tarried at Sinai, would the freshly liberated Hebrew people remember their blessedness, or would they make a golden calf to salve their worrisome souls? Would the people of God believe themselves to be heirs of a promised land, or would they feel like grasshoppers and turn back from Canaan? Would the soldiers of Israel believe themselves to be the army of the living God, or would they slump under the taunts of an overgrown, uncircumcised Philistine?

What will God's people believe about themselves? That's the big question running through the big story of the Bible. The heart of God pulsates with passionate yearning for His people to see their lives from His perspective. Listen to Jesus weep over Zion: "O Jerusalem, Jerusalem, the city that kills the prophets and stones those who are sent to it! How often would I have gathered your children together as a hen gathers her brood under her wings, and you were not willing!" (Matt. 23:37). He might as well have said, "O people of God, I have so wanted to bless you. Why won't you let me show you who you really are?"

I have wept with fathers of anorexic daughters who would give anything for their lovely daughters to believe themselves beautiful. I've groaned with mothers in prayer for their wayward sons to believe themselves heirs, not orphans. God is like a parent yearning for His children to know their worth. He's a Father whose heart breaks when His children believe lies about themselves.

When you become a Christian, it means you believe that God has declared you worth the price of His Son. This goes far to explain why Paul prayed not that we would be more dutiful Christians but that the eyes of our hearts would be enlightened to see the hope of our calling and our glorious inheritance in the saints (Eph. 1:18).

To live a fully blessed life, we must quit reading the Bible as a rule book and start reading it as a revelation of Christ and who we are in Him.

Tired of Being a Tadpole

Ever feel like parts of your life are stuck in the tadpole stage?

I don't know if your list of things you'd like to change about yourself is as long as mine, but we all can feel stuck. I've had besetting defects worse than this, but here's one of my old tadpoles: for many years, I exuded an appearance of success and confidence, but inwardly, I was plagued by insecure, negative thoughts. At best, the anxious thoughts put a ceiling over my life. At worst, the dark reflections cast a heavy shadow over my soul.

As a freshman at the University of North Carolina at Chapel Hill, I was accepted into the honors section of Dr. Grant Wacker's Religion 29, "The History of Christianity in America." It was a large, lecture-style class each Monday and Wednesday, and on Fridays I had the privilege of meeting with Dr. Wacker and about twenty honor students for discussion. But I never spoke. Never. I just swam around, ate my spinach, and kept my gills shut.

My timidity made no sense. On paper, I had the academic résumé for the honors section, but I felt like an imposter. Fearful of asking a stupid question or offering off-target discussion, I just sat there saying nothing until the middle of the semester. When I received my second midterm essay exam back, I was shocked to see I'd scored 98 out of 100. The professor wrote a powerful blessing at the top of the page in red ink: "Alan, anyone who could write an exam like this, nearly flawless work, should have more confidence. Please speak up in class, we need to hear what you have to say."

No amount of telling myself to "just speak up" or "just don't worry about saying something wrong" had ever helped me change. I'd always felt like the basketball player who never wanted the ball in his hands for the last shot. I was consumed with the fear, *What if I miss and become the goat?* I never had the thought, *What if I make it and win the game for the whole team?*

But when Dr. Wacker blessed me in red ink, I slowly started speaking up because I began suspecting that my ideas might indeed be valuable. If you were with me in a classroom discussion today, you'd find it hard to shut me up. I still have too many tadpole mentalities, but when it comes to speaking in front of people, I've become full frog.

One Sunday morning, I shared in a sermon about Professor Wacker's encouraging comment on my midterm, and afterward Lynn Anthony found me. Dr. Anthony is a radiologist in leadership at Wake Forest School of Medicine and is so smart that I can't imagine her ever being a tadpole. Her husband is an elder at our church, and her son is my son's lifelong best friend.

"I have a Grant Wacker story too," she said. Before becoming a doctor, Lynn worked in Christian ministry and studied under Dr. Wacker as part of a master's degree she was pursuing. "Just like you, I wouldn't speak up in class. I grew up in a home where I was taught not to speak unless you were perfectly sure of what you were saying. So I sat silently among the graduate students, until one day Professor Wacker found me in the hall and told me that he knew I had important things to say and he wanted me to speak up. It changed my life."

Evidently, Grant Wacker has helped more than a few tadpoles become frogs. You can too.

Blessing someone is simple:

1. Find a tadpole.
2. Don't scream at it ("Grow some legs!") or shame it ("Have you looked at your tail in the mirror lately?").
3. Show the tadpole a frog.
4. Point to the frog and say, "This is the real you."

Now, if you'll allow me, through the next four chapters I'd like to give you some new lenses so you can see who you really are.

PART TWO

RECEIVING
the BLESSING

4

Blessed to Be Secure

When old Jacob saw his grandsons, the patriarch did something odd and radical: he adopted Ephraim and Manasseh. "Ephraim and Manasseh shall be mine, as Reuben and Simeon are," he said (Gen. 48:5). He made them his heirs. It guaranteed the boys a portion of the promised land, but it also assured the grandsons of something even greater: unconditional acceptance. They knew for sure that they belonged.

That's what blessing does. When we bless, we partner with God to release the essence of His adopting love. Until we are blessed, we are like spiritual orphans looking for assurance. But when we are authentically blessed, it's like being adopted—we know for sure that we are loved. When we are blessed, we become secure. When we become secure, we soar.

Strap 'Em In

Call me "Faster Pastor."

Daniel Britt, general manager of Joy FM, asked me to represent his radio network for an event at the famous Charlotte Motor Speedway called the "Faster Pastor" race.

"Don't worry," Daniel said. "You won't be racing cars. You'll be racing school buses."

I'm not a racer. I've never built a Soap Box Derby car. I've never been to a NASCAR race. I wasn't even good at playing with Hot Wheels as a kid. I've certainly never driven a school bus.

But I said yes.

When my family and I arrived the night of the race, attendants directed us to a special entrance where we drove into the infield of the huge stadium. I gulped when I realized that there were thousands of race fans in the stands that night, and though the "faster pastors" were just a sideshow for the real race event, I soon realized that the other ministers were taking it seriously. Some of them were wearing professional racing suits! Officials gave us a hot dog, a short tour of the epic race car track, and a woefully unsatisfactory orientation.

"Gentlemen, here are your helmets, and there is an earpiece inside so we can talk to you—but you won't be able to talk to us. You're welcome to ride around the infield for a few minutes in order to become comfortable with the air brakes."

I wish there had been time for questions. I had a few, like, "What are air brakes?" and "How do you drive a school bus?" and "Can I go home now?" When I approached my bus I thought, *Why is it so scraped and dented?* After an official strapped me into a five-point harness under a roll bar, the dents started to make sense.

When we lined up for the race, I suddenly felt very old-school Presbyterian—you know, the frozen chosen. I'd been chosen but was frozen in fear. My first thought was to lag toward the rear, avoid all danger, and let a Pentecostal win. But then a strange thought popped into my head: *I'm strapped in with a five-point harness. There's a huge roll bar all around me. I'm probably not going to die tonight. So I might as well put the pedal to the metal.*

When they gave us the green light, my helmet earpiece stopped working and my adrenaline started pumping. I started near the back but began making my move. "Out of the way!" I shouted as I passed the Baptist pastor. "Take that!" I yelled as I edged out a Lutheran. It was wildly exciting. I spun out badly once. They had to tow one severely crashed bus. Preachers were colliding and the fans were hooting. It was more like "Bumper Buses" than "Faster Pastors." I passed about five pastors and finished respectfully in the middle of the pack. I think a Methodist won it. What had started in terror turned into crazy fun *once I felt secure*. It didn't take much—just the tiny revelation *I'm probably not going to die tonight*.

To bless is to strap people into God's love. People only dare greatly when they feel like they're ultimately safe. And they only feel safe when they are unconditionally loved. "There is no fear in love, but perfect love casts out fear. For fear has to do with punishment, and whoever fears has not been perfected in love" (1 John 4:18).

We need to bless others so they'll know that they're strapped into God's love and ours. People can't dare greatly, relax deeply, or enjoy life fully until they know they're secure. The first gift of the Ephraim and Manasseh blessing, like all blessing, is to impart a sense of permanent belonging—the assurance of being accepted fully. When we bless someone, the first thing we do is secure them with the adopting love of God.

Longing for Belonging

Jacob and I have this in common: neither of us was sure our dad really wanted us. Jacob wasn't sure where he stood with his father because "Isaac loved Esau" more than Jacob (Gen. 25:28). I didn't know where I stood with my father because he left when I was in fourth grade and I never knew why. The night he left, Dad told my brothers and me that he loved us. But, paraphrasing Ralph Waldo Emerson, my father's actions thundered so loudly that I couldn't hear what he said. Fourth graders don't understand the complicated dynamics of divorce, so they assume they aren't fully wanted. The unblessed, orphaned heart always feels insecure.

Jacob wanted his father's approval so much that he was willing to become a pretender and settle for a stolen blessing. I understand that too. In my early adult years, I became a people-pleasing perfectionist because, unconsciously, I was trying to win back my dad.

When we pretend to be what others want us to be in order to feel accepted, we settle for a stolen blessing like Jacob. But God longs for us to feel the exhilaration of being wanted regardless of our performance. That's what makes blessing so countercultural and so freeing—when we bless others, we're letting them know that they don't have to posture or pretend anymore.

I think God mandated the Ephraim and Manasseh blessing as a model partly because it starts with adoption, the ultimate strapping into love. The world says, "Perform for me and I'll want you," but God says, "I want you, period." God wants to adopt everyone. He wants everyone to be His heirs. The key to knowing ourselves blessed "with every spiritual blessing" is becoming sure that "in love he predestined us for adoption to himself" (Eph. 1:3–5).

When we bless others, we don't literally adopt them, but we adopt them into our hearts. When we say, "May God make you as Ephraim and Manasseh," we're saying, "You are wanted and accepted like an adopted child. You don't have to worry about being abandoned or rejected. You are secure in God's love." So when we bless, let's always start by finding a way to say, "You're strapped into God's love and mine."

Shiff and Zeni

"God has spoken directly to me three times," my friend Jay Helvey said. "The first was when He told me to leave New York and move to North Carolina. The second was when He directed me to launch a chapter of New Canaan Society men's fellowship in Winston-Salem. And the third was when He told me that we were to adopt internationally." So when Jay and his wife, Jane, decided to adopt two children from an Ethiopian orphanage, they weren't moved by prosperity guilt or some kind of savior mentality. They had been instructed by the Lord. Some of their well-meaning friends tried to talk them out of it, saying, "Why don't you just send money to help children in third-world countries? You're almost fifty—it's crazy."

God Traveled All the Distance

It *was* crazy, of course. Jane is a lovely, gracious community Bible teacher. Jay, who served for years on my ministry board, is a brilliant, prosperous financier who, after an unsuccessful run at Congress, volunteered to launch a fellowship that grew into over a thousand men who've changed our city. Jay and Jane were busy people who had caught a whiff of the more-time-on-your-hands, empty-nest life ahead—but God had a different plan.

International adoption is a long, complicated process that builds nervous anticipation in the parents, until one day it happens. They receive a photo of their future children. It's hard to imagine a moment like that. They had been given a boy named Shiferaw (Shiff) and a girl named Zenebech (Zeni)—Ethiopian twins whose mother had surrendered them to the orphanage not long after they were born. I asked Jay and Jane what they felt when they saw the photo for the first time.

"They looked so sad. I wanted to give them joy," Jane reflected.

Jay grew quiet. His eyes misted. "I just wanted to help them."

Before we know God's love, we're all like Shiff and Zeni, who, while living in an impoverished orphanage, were unaware that seven thousand miles away a man and his wife were weeping over their picture and dreaming of ways to bless them. Though Shiff and Zeni had been orphaned, there was a higher reality at work on their behalf. An invisible force of love and wealth was moving invincibly toward them for their good.

If you are a Christian, it's because your Father set His love on you from eternity and moved heaven and earth to adopt you. He wept over your image, saw your sadness, and sacrificed everything to help you. "In this is love, not that we have loved God but that he loved us" (1 John 4:10). When you bless people, you help them envision how much God has always wanted them, and you remind them how far He traveled to claim them.

God's Picture Book

Jay and his son Cole went for a visit to the orphanage months before the Ethiopian siblings would be officially released into the Helveys' care.

"Papi!" Shiff exclaimed when he saw Jay. It was the only English word he knew. Though Jay knew no Amharic, he had brought a photo album featuring photos of Shiff and Zeni's big new house and their new big brothers. The book had pictures of the yard, the dogs, the neighborhood, and the city. After their visit, Jay left the book and promised (through a translator), "I'll be back to get you and take you home with me."

I wonder how Shiff and Zeni felt in the interim days as they gazed at the book of pictures about their home in America. It's a hard thing to live in two worlds. It's not easy to remember that you have a benevolent papi making plans for you when you're still sleeping on an orphanage cot.

If you walk with God long enough, you'll have days when it's hard to feel His presence, and there will be some days when you'll find yourself just holding on to the Book and clinging to His promises. In a lot of ways, the Bible is your family photo album. It's a vivid collection of pictures of who you are in Christ and where you're headed. When people feel like orphans, they don't need us to use the Bible to tell them how they ought to act. They need us to bless them with Scriptures that remind them of who God is, who they are, and what a glorious future is ahead.

Orphans don't need someone to tell them to try harder; they need someone to adopt them and show them pictures of a new life ahead. Spiritual orphans don't need law; they need grace. "It's a cruel jest," Martin Luther King Jr. said, "to say to a bootless man that he ought to lift himself by his own bootstraps."[1] So Shiff and Zeni waited for their boots, and as they waited, they held on to the pictures and promises, until one day Jay and Jane arrived to take them home.

America!

Fittingly, Jay and Jane picked up Shiff and Zeni the day after they celebrated the resurrection. It was Easter Monday 2008.

"After all the planning, paperwork, and waiting, they just hand you the kids and say, 'Here you go,'" Jane said.

"All they had were the clothes on their backs and the photo album," Jay added. He chuckled when he said, "And the orphanage asked us to send the clothes back to them once we had bought some new ones."

When God adopts you, you come empty-handed. You don't come into His family clothed with any merit of your own. You don't bring any of your own righteousness to the story. "For by grace you have been saved through faith. And this is not your own doing; it is the gift of God, not a result of works, so that no one may boast" (Eph. 2:8–9). When God adopts you, He provides the wardrobe: "He has clothed me with the garments of salvation; he has covered me with the robe of righteousness" (Isa. 61:10).

It took days for the paperwork to clear, so the Helveys took their four-year-olds to the Sheraton in Addis Ababa. It's a luxurious hotel with marbled floors, sumptuous restaurants, and lavish grounds. I wish I could have witnessed Shiff and Zeni see it all for the first time.

"They'd never seen an elevator. They just wanted to keep pushing the buttons," Jane said.

"They'd never seen green grass, much less chandeliers and a swimming pool," Jay added. "It was a delight to see it all through their eyes."

When you love people, you take joy in watching them discover wonders you've already seen many times. I had seen the Grand Canyon twice before we took our kids to see it. When I saw the canyon for the first time, my jaw dropped. But watching my kids' faces when they saw it for the first time moved me more than the canyon ever did. Blessing people is like taking Ethiopian twins to see their first green lawn or restaurant or pool. Your words can paint pictures of others' lives more glorious than any marbled hotel and grander than any canyon.

During the long months of waiting, staff at the orphanage often looked at the picture book with the kids and told them, "This is your new home in America." So Shiff and Zeni knew two English words: "Papa" and "America." If the Ethiopian twins had flown across the ocean to live in a double-wide mobile home in rural North Carolina, it would have seemed like a palace to them. But the Helveys brought Shiff and

Zeni to a beautiful, stately house in one of Winston-Salem's loveliest neighborhoods. After the long trip, when they finally pulled up in front of their new house, Shiff grinned and shouted, "America!"

Shiff and Zeni would soon learn that America is more than a house and adoption means more than provision. What they would discover is what we all need if we are going to thrive in this world: security. When blessing is withheld, we become unsure and lag behind in fear, but when we are assured that we're loved, we put the pedal to the metal.

How Trust Is Born

When you were a baby, you couldn't do any family chores, contribute to the household income, or impress anyone. You only knew how to cry, drink milk, and wet your diaper. Despite your helplessness and neediness, if you had a healthy mother, she took you in her arms and nursed you thousands of times in love. And there, in the arms of unconditional love, is where you learned to trust. That's why David declared of the Lord, "You . . . led me to trust you at my mother's breast" (Ps. 22:9 NLT).

Until the mid-twentieth century, experts encouraged parents not to overly coddle their infants for fear that the children would become spoiled. But in the 1950s, psychologist Harry Harlow shook such ideologies with his famous, controversial experiments with rhesus monkeys. In the classic study, Harlow showed that, given a choice, baby monkeys preferred a pretend cloth mother that provided nothing but its soft feel rather than a stark, wire surrogate mother that provided milk but no contact comfort. The babies with wire "mothers" had trouble digesting the milk and were prone to diarrhea. When a baby monkey was separated from its cloth mother for three days, the infant rhesus wasn't toughened up by its adventure in independence but instead became scared, insecure, and clingy upon its return to the mother. The baby monkeys that only had wire surrogate mothers were generally insecure in unfamiliar surroundings and had little courage to explore.

Though some of his practices were criticized, Harlow's work was widely accepted as conclusive evidence that abundant parental affection was likely not to spoil the child but to strengthen the child. The more parental contact, the healthier the child.

It is not the withholding of love but the assurance of love that causes us to flourish. In fact, the more we feel guaranteed of deep affection, the more likely we are to become confident explorers and conquerors in life.

A lot of parents, teachers, coaches, and preachers think that lavish blessing will demotivate their children, students, or parishioners. Knowing that people will work hard in an effort to be accepted, authorities often withhold acceptance like a dangling carrot. There's an enormous problem with such a strategy—it's motivation by fear. When we're afraid and insecure, like the rhesus monkeys separated from their cloth mothers, we become hesitant, clingy, and upset. When the blessing is withheld, it produces a destructive cycle that looks like this:

Simply put, to withhold blessing is to withhold acceptance. When we withhold our acceptance of others, we make them more insecure. But God wants to do the opposite. He wants everyone to become secure in His love.

Someone has estimated that there are 365 "fear not" statements in the Bible—one for every day of the year. God hates fear but loves faith: "Without faith it is impossible to please him" (Heb. 11:6). When we bless others, we participate with God to break the worldly cycle of fear in order to create a transformational new pattern that looks like this:

Adopted by God

> For you did not receive the spirit of slavery to fall back into fear, but you have received the Spirit of adoption as sons, by whom we cry, "Abba! Father!" (Rom. 8:15)

The primary New Testament image for becoming a Christian is adoption. To be a Christian is to be adopted by God as His heir, permanently secure in His love. Interestingly, the backdrop for the New Testament image isn't the adoption of infants. It's the Roman practice of adopting young adults to become heirs.

Historians have clear records about adoption practices in the early Roman Empire. An affluent first-century Roman who had no son could adopt a young man to become his heir. Often, he would adopt a slave. The process of adoption from slave to son was a serious matter of Roman law called *adrogation*, from the Latin word for "ask," *rogatur*. Legal officials solemnly *asked* the adopting father (the adrogator) if he indeed desired the young man (the adrogatus) to become his lawful son. According to Justinian's *Institutes*:

1. All debts owed by the adrogatus were extinguished upon adoption.
2. The adrogatus lost all legal standing with his old family.
3. Though Roman law allowed a father to disown a biological son, it was unlawful to ever disown an adopted son.

Let that sink in. An adopted child could never be rejected. Once God adopts you, it cannot be reversed. You're strapped in. You're safe forever. You're wanted forever. You're accepted forever.

When our kids were babies, I sang a blessing to them as they fell asleep. I sang a blessing to them before they could comprehend the words because I wanted it to go deep into their spirits. I sang to Bennett, "You are my baby boy. Your father really loves you—oh, how much he loves you. Never will he leave you, never will he deceive you, and always, always, he will believe in you. You are, and always will be, my baby boy." I sang a different blessing to Abby every night: "There will never be a time when you'll lose this love of mine—it will always be. There will never be a day when my love will go away—it will always be. There will never be an hour when my love will lose its power—it will always be. There will never be a minute when my love won't have you in it—it will always be. Your father's love will always be holding you."

When we sing our blessing to others, we mustn't change our song when they don't yet act the way we want them to act. Until they're secure in love, they're prone to act out their insecurities. Jane Helvey remembers one of her new twins biting her arm one day. It takes time for adopted orphans to believe themselves heirs.

Is there someone in your life who is acting insecurely? Have you tried blessing them? If you haven't seen results yet, don't change your tune. Don't ever stop blessing an orphan even if at first they bite. Keep strapping 'em into God's love.

Mine

Ephraim and Manasseh shall be mine, as Reuben and Simeon are. (Gen. 48:5)

Old Jacob didn't want Ephraim and Manasseh ever to feel insecure like he had for most of his life, so he adopted them. Most of us aren't literal orphans, but most of us are spiritual orphans. We need to be blessed if we are ever going to feel like we truly belong. If we belong to a club or a gang or a team because of our skills or commitment, we know our membership is fragile. If we fail or fall, we can be kicked out of the club.

That's why blessing is utterly countercultural and absolutely essential. We need to know we belong—that we are wanted—not because we've proven ourselves but just because we exist.

If you want to bless others with a sense of security, first come before God the Father, see His smile, feel His affection, and hear Him say, "I've chosen you—I want to make you mine." Say yes to your adoption in Christ. Say yes to your inheritance. Say yes to all the assurances of God's Word. Declare Ephesians 1:3–4 daily: "I'm blessed with every spiritual blessing because He chose me in Him before the foundation of the world."

We're never too old to be blessed by a deep sense of belonging.

My friend Dean Weaver somehow has a heart big enough to pastor the sizable Memorial Park Church in the suburbs of Pittsburgh and father a seemingly ever-growing family. In addition to their three biological children, Dean and his wife adopted two children from Sierra Leone and one from the West Indies.

With all six kids grown, Dean and his wife got to know a young African American man named Tommy who was interning for a college ministry in their community. Tommy's dad struggled with drugs and his mother wasn't always available, so when Tommy needed a place to stay, big-hearted Dean and his wife welcomed Tommy into their home like one of their own.

Tommy was a scholarship collegiate basketball athlete. He's articulate and has a master's degree and a heart for ministry, so he has a lot in common with Dean. Still, it's not something you see every day—a six-foot-eight-inch, twenty-four-year-old black guy moving into a fifty-six-year-old white pastor's house. But the Weaver family isn't like most families.

"What *is* this?" Tommy asked Dean one day as he looked around at the multiethnic family that had welcomed him so openly.

"Well," Dean said, "this is a family. This is a mom and a dad and kids. This is what we are—and we love doing it. And we love having you around."

When it came time for Tommy to head off for a ministry position in Memphis, he had a question for Dean: "It's time for me to renew my driver's license. I don't really have an address to give them. What should I do?"

"Put down our Pittsburgh address," Dean said. "Then, when you look at your license, you'll always remember where you can find some good home cooking. And by the way, if you come back at Christmas, there will be some presents under the tree for you."

When Tommy came to the Weaver home for Christmas, Dean approached him with an offer: "I've investigated it. In Pennsylvania, there is no age limit for adoption. Tommy, the whole family has talked about it and we'd like to legally adopt you. We want you to be a permanent part of the family."

Tommy said he'd like to think and pray about it.

When Dean saw Tommy next, he asked his prospective son if he'd considered their offer. Tommy said that he had. He rolled up his shirtsleeve, and tattooed on his arm was his answer. It read simply, "Weaver."

The blessing everyone needs most is to know they belong. Everyone needs to be adopted by God. Thankfully, there's no age limit for joining the family. There's no limit to the Father's heart, no restriction of space in the kingdom. When you bless others, you remind them of that and help them believe in the permanence of God's adopting love. When you bless people, you tattoo the name of God on their hearts.

5

Blessed to Be Free

As I write, my sweet, remarkably strong eighty-six-year-old mom is battling pancreatic cancer. When doctors diagnosed it over two years ago, my two brothers and I joined her for a three-hour, interdisciplinary clinic at Forsyth Medical Center. We met the medical professionals one after the other—the radiation oncologist, the medical oncologist, the surgeon, the nutritionist, the geneticist, and the nurse navigator. Afterward, we shed some tears and my mom said, "I don't want to talk about it anymore today." So we went to a nice lunch.

Our son, Bennett, and his wife drove to town to join us. They brought Nana flowers, and we ate good food, talked about all the grandkids, and laughed a lot. When I dropped Mom back at her house that evening, she smiled and said, "Thanks. This has been such a good day."

A good day? My mother is a woman of profound faith, but how could anyone be *that* positive? How could a day of chemo and radiation planning be a *good* day?

She had so filled her heart with hope that the cancer diagnosis took a back seat. The love of family had, at least for the moment, made her forget her troubles.

If blessing is powerful enough, it can overshadow yesterday's sorrows thoroughly enough to eclipse the pain. That's how God wants us to live. He wants us so assured of His power to forgive and restore that we never spend a moment bogged down in regret. Through the power of blessing, it's possible to live as though we've forgotten all our failures and disappointments. The name Manasseh in Jacob's blessing points the way.

Joseph's first thirty years were marked by horrendous pain and trouble. His brothers hated him, threw him into a pit, and sold him into slavery. His slave master's wife falsely accused him of attempted rape, and the master threw Joseph into prison. As far as he knew, Joseph would never see his family again. Hated, rejected, abused, enslaved, and falsely imprisoned, Joseph faced crushing troubles. But by a series of providential events, Pharaoh elevated the wise, young Hebrew dream interpreter. God exalted Joseph in Egypt in order to save the world from famine.

There, as ruler in a foreign land, Joseph married the daughter of a priest, and they had a son. "Joseph named his firstborn Manasseh and said, 'It is because God has made me forget all my trouble'" (Gen. 41:51 NIV). In Hebrew, *Manasseh* sounds like the word "forget." Of course, Joseph didn't literally forget all his troubles—the narrative of his reunion with his brothers makes that clear. But he forgot his pain the way a mother "forgets" the pain of childbirth—the elation of holding her baby overshadows the labor pains.

We live in a world that is quick to dredge up our failures and pain. When we mess up, even people close to us might say things like, "You always act that way" or "I remember how you messed up the other time." Curse wants to resurface old shame to create a sense of doom for today. Blessing does the opposite—it liberates in order to create hope for tomorrow. Blessing, like all love, "keeps no record of wrongs" (1 Cor. 13:5 NIV) and finds a thousand ways to say, "Yesterday is over. A new day has dawned for you." The Manasseh part of the Ephraim and Manasseh blessing tells people, "Your past troubles do not have to define you, but they can *refine* you."

How Abby Found Her Smile

We have a framed family photo taken in 2001 at the Chef Mickey restaurant at a Disney World resort that I want to keep even though three-year-old Abby isn't smiling. She's dolled up in a Minnie costume at the "happiest place on earth" and isn't smiling because she hardly ever grinned for the first several years of her life. We named her after David's wife in the Bible, who was an "intelligent and beautiful woman" (1 Sam. 25:3 NIV) because Abigail, in Hebrew, means "my father's joy."

In the years leading up to our daughter's birth, our lives had been flooded with joy. Anne and I had experienced a spiritual renewal that had filled our lives with laughter and celebration. Our son, Bennett, born four years prior to Abby, came into a silly, lighthearted home where we rolled on the carpet and giggled. I'd rub my nose on baby Bennett's bare tummy, and he'd cackle. Sometimes we'd hear him on the baby monitor, chuckling at the sight of the mobile above his crib.

Soon after Abby was born, a squall blew into our home and our climate of joy turned into an atmosphere of dark sadness. My wife's best friend was her baby sister, Mary, who, with her husband and four little children, lived near us. It's hard to describe how much Anne loved her sister. I think when Mary was born, Anne thought God had given her a live doll. And Mary was a doll—beautiful, fun, and as sweet as the sugary part of the Moravian sugar cake she would steal from me on Christmas Day. I loved her as much as if she were my own sister.

Abby was born at the end of September 1998, and Mary hesitated to hold her niece because she had been coughing a lot. Doctors assumed it was a stubborn virus. By Thanksgiving, Mary hurt so badly that she stayed on the couch most of the day. Doctors thought it was fibromyalgia and sent her to the pain clinic. But when she saw a pulmonologist in December, the dark tempest arrived—it was lung cancer, in a thirty-three-year-old mother of four who had never smoked a cigarette in her life. By the time they found it, the cancer had invaded her bones. Within a year, our sweet Mary died. Our grief ran deeper than words.

Three months after Abby was born, Anne's other sister, Katherine, gave birth to Zach, whose special needs required multiple surgeries, hospital stays, and diligent attention for his risk of seizures night and day.

Two months after Mary's death, a sedan ran a stop sign at full speed and broadsided Anne's station wagon, crushing and upending it and causing Anne a year of therapy for her leg. A little more than a year after Mary's death, Anne also began experiencing troubling medical symptoms. Doctors diagnosed it as the onset of a potentially debilitating neurological disease. My father became quite ill during those days and required my regular attention. Our church was understaffed at the time, and I worked sixty hours a week trying to manage a major conflict brewing in the congregation while also trying to meet a book deadline.

I recount all the suffering to explain why, during the formative first year of her life, Abby nursed in the arms of a sobbing mother. It explains why we can't find any baby pictures of Abby smiling.

Several miracles and several years later, our laughter slowly returned. We had grieved Mary's death in a healthy way. The Lord sustained Anne's physical health. Zach survived by God's grace. Anne and I were smiling again, but Abby wasn't. The great sadness that we had weathered had imprinted on her infant soul. She had joy in her name but not in her heart.

We never said, "Oh well, Abby is going to be our melancholy child." Instead, we decided to bless her every day for who she was designed to be—her father's joy. We began speaking the psalmist's words about the "oil of gladness" (Ps. 45:7) over her life, and we announced the messianic promise of Isaiah assuring us of "a garment of praise instead of a spirit of despair" (Isa. 61:3 NIV). I sang a blessing to her every night. I regularly placed my hands on her small frame as she slept in her crib and blessed her destiny of joy. If Abby cracked even a tiny smile, we celebrated. If she laughed, we'd laugh with her even harder. Every day I reminded her of her name. "You're Abigail—it means 'my father's joy.' You're a child of joy, and you bring us all such great joy."

We weren't trying to veer Abby away from her given nature. We were blessing her toward her true self.

I can't point to the day it happened. A miracle just slowly, surely unfolded. Abby became a child of joy. She started wrestling and giggling with Bennett and me. She discovered the delight of a belly laugh. And she grew into a wise and beautiful woman of great joy. I wish you could meet her. I wish you could see how much she loves life and people. I wish you could hear the way she spins a joke and see the way she can light up a room. By the power of blessing, Abby has forgotten all the troubles she was born into. She ought to be a Disney princess.

The City Will Be Rebuilt on Her Ruins

When Bennett was a boy, we gave him a remote-controlled helicopter for Christmas. Well, in hindsight, I gave *us* a remote-controlled helicopter for Christmas. It was a black Aviator RC, a real beauty. Bennett was eager to fly it, but I was more eager. We decided to wait until our winter beach trip for the chopper's maiden flight. Like Orville and Wilbur Wright, Alan and Bennett Wright walked bravely through North Carolina coastal dunes with aircraft in hand. I wanted to go first but acquiesced after whining a bit. Bennett flew the chopper with skill above the dunes, negotiating the beach winds carefully and returning the helicopter safely. It looked exhilarating.

"Bennett," I pleaded, "can I have a turn now?"

"I don't know, Dad. I'm afraid you'll lose control of it. It's not so easy."

"Oh, come on. How hard can it be? Please!"

Reluctantly, he turned the remote control over to me.

"That's high enough," Bennett exclaimed as I directed the helicopter higher than he had. *"Dad!"*

I don't know what happened.

It was like a drug. I couldn't stop myself. I had to fly it higher. The wind flung the helicopter fifty yards away as the controller shook in my hands. With no contact with the remote control, the toy was at the mercy of the beach winds. We watched helplessly as the Aviator slammed into the side of a three-story oceanfront house and shattered into pieces. My flight was shorter than the Wrights' at Kitty Hawk.

I wished the wind would blow me away too, out to sea. Perhaps that would be easier than facing my son. Instead, Bennett and I walked silently to the crash site. We both knew the helicopter was beyond repair. Bennett didn't say anything. He just went inside to be alone.

After giving him a moment, I followed Bennett inside. What does a father say when he's shattered his son's new toy helicopter?

"I'm going to get you another one."

A loving father longs to restore his child's broken dreams. You can hear the father heart of God in Jeremiah's words to the people of God stuck in exile in Babylon:

This is what the LORD says: "I will restore the fortunes of Jacob's tents and have compassion on his dwellings; the city will be rebuilt on her ruins, and the palace will stand in its proper place." (Jer. 30:18 NIV)

"I will restore"—that's God's longing. God grieves the brokenness of the exiles. He takes no delight in your troubles. He mourns your broken dreams and has compassion for your travails.

"The city will be rebuilt on her ruins" is my favorite phrase in Jeremiah's prophecy. In ancient Palestine, marauding armies would often level a city, leaving it in ruins. The army would capture or kill the citizens and leave the city's walls and buildings crumbled in a heap—a mound of rubble. Over time, the winds would blow and the desert sands would settle into the rubble. After years of sedimentary buildup, the old city's ruins would be filled in with dirt and sand, creating a big hill called a "tel." What once were useless ruins over time became a prime, strategically elevated building site for a new city. Returning citizens or new settlers would often rebuild the city atop the tel, giving them a higher perspective and a safer, more strategically located city. They literally rebuilt the city on her ruins.

When you bless those who have been marauded by life, you can help them see the "tel" that has emerged from their rubble. I never would have voted for the family of my childhood to break, but because of that familial rubble, God has given me a ministry to the broken. I never would have voted for the shame of growing up in a home besieged by alcohol abuse, but because of the debris, God has given me a voice for those in shame. I never would have voted for the grief of a sister's death, but because of the ruins, I'm unafraid to be with others in their mourning.

What does your rubble look like? Your city can be rebuilt on your ruins.

The Blessings That Heal

Ever wondered why Jesus wept with the mourners at Lazarus's tomb even though He knew He was going to raise Martha and Mary's brother from the dead (John 11:33–35)? Empathy heals. Scholar and author Brené Brown has proven the power of empathy over shame and explains that when we empathize, we don't feel sorry for someone, we feel *with* someone. Empathy, Brown says, is "the ability to tap into our own experiences in order to connect with an experience someone is relating to us."[1] The voice of empathy never hears a friend's troubles and says, "Well, at least you never . . ." or "Well, it could be worse." The voice of empathy says simply, "I'm not sure what to say, but I hear your hurt and I'm with you." We're tempted, like Job's friends, to give hurting people advice. We want to give people a to-do list in order to "fix" them.

Blessing is the opposite. Blessing isn't advice—it's grace put into words. Let's explore some of the ways we can bless with empathy those who've seen troubles like Joseph.

1) "Yes, Eileen . . . It's Real"

When you're hurting, sometimes the blessing you need most is someone else's reassuring faith. The voice of curse shames hurting people about their wavering faith, but blessing says, "I have faith on your behalf." When you bless others in pain, you don't highlight their doubts—you extend your own trust in God.

Eileen McClure is a gentle deaconess in her seventies with a soft voice and a deep reservoir of wisdom. She cared compassionately for her dementia-ridden husband,

Lowell, for six years until his death. She has walked through suffering with awe-inspiring patience. When someone in our church suffers deep loss, I like Eileen to visit them. She is one of the most empathetic people I've ever known.

In October of 2004, Eileen and Lowell's world crumbled when they learned that their son Joey, two months shy of his graduation from Appalachian State University in Boone, North Carolina, had been murdered. When I went to the McClures' home that night, it felt like the oxygen was missing from the air. That level of pain is suffocating. Joey grew up in our youth group. Everybody loved him. A thug had shot him and left him by a gravel road.

Going back to church can be hard for those in grief. It can be hard to sing songs of praise when your soul is smothered with lament. But Eileen and Lowell started going back to church a few weeks after the funeral. As she exited the sanctuary that day, she paused, looked at me numbly, and asked, "Pastor, is it true?"

She was asking me if the gospel I had just proclaimed was true. She was asking me if I really believed what I preached—that God is good, Jesus is alive, and heaven exists.

"Yes, Eileen. It's true. It's real—all of it is true."

She had to ask me because a woman in that kind of pain can't reassure herself. Every week, she would walk out of church and ask me, "Pastor, is it true?" And I'd look her in the eye and say, "Yes, Eileen, it's all true." She asked me every week for several years until she had less need to ask. Today, more than sixteen years after the tragedy, sometimes she'll ask me again, "Is it real?" But now she smiles a little because she knows it's true.

When we bless people, we don't tell them what they "ought" to believe—we tell them the good news that *we* believe for them.

2) "God Sees You"

Blessing doesn't explain the logic of God. It bears witness to the love of God. Though it's bizarre and inexplicable, our all-powerful God often allows His children to experience hardship while supernaturally attending to them in the midst of their suffering. God could have liberated Joseph from slavery, but instead, "the LORD was with Joseph, and he became a successful man, and he was in the house of his Egyptian master" (Gen. 39:2). God could have kept him from the dungeon, but "the LORD was with Joseph and showed him steadfast love and gave him favor in the sight of the keeper of the prison" (Gen. 39:21). Blessing doesn't explain suffering. Blessing points to God's presence in the midst of the suffering.

In the midst of our great sadness when Mary was fighting cancer, well-known author Jack Deere came to our church for a repeat visit. Jack had become a personal mentor and had imparted rich inspiration and wisdom to our church. During his visit in the spring of 2000, Jack brought a lay minister from his church, a real estate developer named Carl Greer who is uniquely gifted in blessing. It's a beautiful thing to watch Carl minister. He's a gentle man who often weeps empathetically as he encourages people in revelatory ways. Carl had never met Anne or me until that week, but as he and Jack concluded our worship gathering one evening, he wanted to share a blessing publicly with Anne.

He looked to the front pew where my wife and I sat. "Anne, I feel like God has shown me something, and I wonder if it would be all right to share it with you. I don't want to be too forward, but I think it will encourage you."

Anne swallowed hard and nodded.

"I saw you in your bedroom kneeling and praying. You were crying out to God. I think God wants you to know that He hears you and He's with you. You're a woman of deep prayer, and God sees you."

Anne didn't normally kneel when she prayed, but during the recent searing days of adversity, she had started spending time in the bedroom on her knees. As Carl spoke, my beautiful, adversity-stricken wife wept. His blessing nourished her deeply.

But in the days after Jack and Carl left, Anne began to doubt. *He could have said those words to almost anyone*, she thought. The power of Carl's blessing began to dim.

A few weeks earlier, Anne and I had visited the local Christian bookstore in search of a book I needed. While there, for some reason Anne plucked a single book from the hundreds on the shelves. She'd never read anything by the author, Ken Gire, but the title captured her attention: *The Reflective Life.*

"I'd like to get this book," she said.

"Honey," I whined, "we came to get a book *I* need."

"I *really* want this book," she said. "I'm going to get it." So she did.

She savored it like a delicacy. Every night for weeks, she'd read *The Reflective Life* in bed, and as I was trying to fall asleep, she'd say, "Listen to this passage. . . . Isn't this good?"

It *was* good. Nothing nourished her more during her sister's sickness than Ken Gire's book.

A week after Carl and Jack left, Carl sent us a package. Inside was a note:

> Dear Anne, I'm praying for you regularly. Thank you for your hospitality during my visit. Upon my return, the Lord put a book on my heart that I thought you might like. I hope it nourishes you.

Inside the package was a copy of *The Reflective Life*.

When we saw it, we just grew quiet and wept. God was with us in our pain.

God was with Joseph in the slave master's house. God was with Joseph in the prison.

You may never know a reason for your suffering, but you can know this for sure: God is with you in the midst of it. Blessing doesn't say, "Here's how God is using this suffering in your life" as much as it says, "I see God right there with you." It's not a blessing when you try to explain someone's pain. People don't need you to make sense of their adversity—they need you to help them see God in the midst of it.

3) There Is No Condemnation in Christ

The best blessing we can give to someone who has failed is forgiveness. Blessing always wants others to see their lives in the light of grace. The voice of curse says, "You're stuck because of your past failures." Blessing heralds Paul's famous crescendo: "There is therefore now no condemnation for those who are in Christ Jesus" (Rom. 8:1).

I chuckle every time I think of the little boy named Johnny and his sister, who were visiting their grandmother one summer at her rural home. One day, unthinkingly, Johnny shot their grandmother's pet-like duck with his BB gun and killed it. The horrified boy covered up his crime as best he could. After supper that evening, the grandmother announced to Johnny's sister that it was her night to clean the dishes.

"Johnny said he wanted to do the dishes tonight, Grandma." She leaned over and whispered in Johnny's ear, "I saw what you did to the duck."

So Johnny did the dishes.

The next morning after breakfast, his sister said again, "Johnny would like to do the breakfast dishes also." Then she whispered to her brother, "Remember the duck."

This manipulation went on for days. Big sister continually whispered, "Remember the duck," and Johnny did all the chores. Finally Johnny couldn't take it anymore and said, "I can't stand it! Grandmother, I shot your duck with my BB gun and killed it. I'm sorry."

"I know, Johnny," she said. "I saw the whole thing, and I've been wondering how long you were going to let your sister hold it over your head."

How long has the voice of shame been holding your old "ducks" over your head?

Legend has it that Soviet dictator Joseph Stalin had a psychologist whose torture techniques never failed. The torture expert explained his strategy with a story. There once was a peasant who appeared in the royal court before an important official. The peasant sat before a big red button atop a huge mahogany desk. "If you push this red button," the official told him, "an old man will die in Mongolia, and we will pay you a million rubles." After agonizing over the decision and being assured that the old man in Mongolia deserved to die, the peasant pushed the button. But he was never able to enjoy his wealth because he was haunted by what he'd done.

"Everyone has one of those red buttons in their past," Stalin's psychologist asserted. "My job is to find out what it is and resurface it over and over until the mind is tortured into telling me whatever I want."

The antidote to the red button torture is forgiveness.

The former head of psychiatry at Duke, Dr. Bill Wilson, was a friend—a brilliant psychiatrist who loved Jesus and spoke bluntly. I once heard him tell about a dying patient who needed a miracle. The Vietnam vet had been hospitalized for weeks, suffering from multiple life-threatening maladies, but his soul seemed more tortured than his body. One day, he confessed that he was riddled with unbearable shame.

"Has it ever occurred to you," Dr. Wilson asked, "that you could be forgiven?"

"No," the patient muttered. "I can't be forgiven. You don't know what I've done."

The psychiatrist sat down, and the veteran told his story. Years ago in Vietnam he'd gotten bored and done target practice on a Vietnamese woman—an innocent citizen. Ever since, he'd been tortured with guilt, and his physical and mental health had declined.

Dr. Wilson's blessing was simple: "God already knows about your crime, and He loves you. You can be forgiven."

Then Bill Wilson described the miracle. First, the patient accepted God's love, and then, step-by-step, his body followed suit and was healed.

Curse kills. Blessing gives life by finding a thousand ways to say, "There is therefore now no condemnation for you in Christ."

There's Gold in Your Broken Places

Since the fifteenth century, the Japanese have made pottery repair an art form. Master artisans use a technique called *kintsugi* ("golden joinery") to mend broken ceramics with gold-dusted lacquer. The golden glue in the repaired vessel makes the pottery more beautiful because it holds together its story. The ancient art of kintsugi affirms that the vessel's broken history is part of its beauty. Kintsugi doesn't try to hide the pottery's troubled history. It uses gold to make the once-broken, now-mended vessel more valuable than before. When you look at a bowl repaired with the kintsugi technique, the randomness of the golden seams is lovely. You don't look at the bowl and say, "Oh dear, it is previously broken pottery." You look at it and say, "What a beautiful vessel."

I think that's what it means to bless people to be like Manasseh. It doesn't mean that we help them forget their troubles by denying the brokenness of the past or the suffering of today. Our blessing is more like golden kintsugi glue. The mended life we have in Christ isn't a cover-up of our troubles—it's a restoration job.

Joseph's life was fractured by rejection, abuse, enslavement, and wrongful incarceration, but God mended his life with gold. No one reads the story of Joseph and says, "He's the broken, troubled kid." Instead, everyone says, "He's the one who ruled in Egypt, saved the world, and forgave his brothers."

Your troubles aren't the end of your story. You're a kintsugi vessel whose fractures are mended by the gold of God's grace. Your real story is in the golden seams.

6

Blessed to Be Twice Fruitful

I coached Bennett's childhood soccer team for years because no one else would do it. When they were trying to find a coach, I hid the fact that I'd played right wing on a high school state championship team. (I didn't score very often and had a weak left leg and substandard stamina.) But word got out that I had some soccer experience, and, well, the team was going to disband if I didn't take it over.

Thankfully, we were in the less competitive Optimist Club league. The head of the organization was a retired Quaker minister who, at the mandatory coaches' orientation, told us, "The kids just want to kick the ball and eat a snack. So your job is to make sure that every kid gets to kick the ball and that you always have a snack after the game."

The team I inherited was very good at eating the snack but terrible at kicking the ball. The first season we won only one game.

My ever-positive, sweet wife tried to be encouraging. Before every game she'd say to Bennett, "Remember, sweetie, it's not whether you win or lose that matters—all that matters is having fun." That was the sum total of her weekly pregame pep talk: "Remember, Bennett . . ."

It got so he'd interrupt, "I know, Mom. It doesn't matter whether we win or lose as long as we're having fun."

"That's right, sweetie. So go have some fun and don't forget to take the snacks."

After losing about five games in a row, I told my happy, noncompetitive wife, "Sweetheart, I appreciate your positive words, and I know I tend to be too competitive, but would you please quit saying, 'It doesn't matter whether you win or lose'? That's not really what I want to teach the boys. I'd like to do *some* winning."

I went on to explain that, while I understand that males tend to be overly competitive and too many people idolize success, these boys were going to have to grow up and live in a world of competition. If one of these boys grew up to be a corporate salesman, his boss probably wouldn't send him out saying, "Remember, it's not whether you make a sale or not—it's just about having fun." And if that salesman came home dejected one day because he lost his major account and didn't know how he was going to pay the bills, it wouldn't help if his wife said, "Well, as long as you had fun today, dear."

Anne smiled and said she understood. Over the years, our team got better at kicking the ball. My last year coaching, we went undefeated. Everyone discovered that the snacks always taste better after you win.

It's a very tricky thing to bless people for their success because, especially in American culture, people seem to care more about the results than the process. How can you bless someone to win without idolizing the trophy? How can you bless others to be their best without exalting America's false gods of success?

May You Be Twice Fruitful

> The name of the second he called Ephraim, "For God has made me fruitful in the land of my affliction." (Gen. 41:52)

As we learned in the last chapter, Joseph named his first-born son Manasseh because God's blessing had so overwhelmed Joseph's sorrows that it was as if he'd forgotten all his troubles. When Joseph's second son was born, he named him Ephraim because God hadn't just sustained Joseph in the midst of his afflictions. God had also made Joseph surprisingly fruitful. Everything Joseph touched had prospered.

The name literally translated is "Ephrayim." Unlike English, the Hebrew language has singular, plural, and dual nouns. Dual words end with the Hebrew suffix *ayim*—it usually connotes two of something. For example, the Hebrew word for "day" is *yom*. The word for "two days" is *yom-ayim*. When Joseph named his second son, he combined the Hebrew verb meaning "to bear fruit" with the dual suffix *ayim* to form the name "Ephrayim" (pronounced *ef-rah´-yim*). Ephraim is the dual form of *fruitful*—"doubly fruitful."

In part, the name references the double blessing of bearing two sons. But I think the prophetically gifted Joseph meant something more far-reaching in the name. He knew that God had made him twice as fruitful as he'd ever imagined. When we bless people to be like Ephraim, we're saying, "May God make you twice as fruitful as you could ever be by your own power."

I used to think it was more spiritual not to care about results. I had heard preachers and teachers say things like, "God doesn't care whether you're successful, just whether you're obedient." Part of the reason I used to think it was nobler to care about obedience than results is the excess we've all seen. When preachers imply that if we give to their ministry, God will make us wealthy, it's unbiblical and manipulative. When preachers suggest that if we have enough faith, we'll never be sick, in trouble, or sad, it not only is unscriptural but also leads to disillusionment, because as Jesus made clear, "In the world you will have tribulation" (John 16:33).

All that said, Jesus never taught, "It doesn't matter whether you get any results as long as you're having fun." God *does* care about how fruitful we are. He blessed Adam and Eve so that they could "be fruitful and multiply" (Gen. 1:28). The old covenant unveiled His heart to prosper His people: "He will love you, bless you, and multiply you. He will also bless the fruit of your womb and the fruit of your ground, your grain and your wine and your oil, the increase of your herds and the young of your flock" (Deut. 7:13). When the Lord sent His people into the promised land, He intended for them to win every battle (Josh. 1:3). Jesus clearly wanted His disciples to be fruitful: "By this my Father is glorified, that you bear much fruit" (John 15:8). He talked about seed bearing a hundredfold return (Matt. 13:8) and commended servants who invested their talents for a fruitful return (Matt. 25:14–30).

Blessed People Bless People

The most important fruit anyone can bear is love. It's the first in Paul's list of spiritual fruit (Gal. 5:22–23). According to Jesus, love is the summation of all the law (Matt. 22:40). I found out early on that if I wanted my children to act lovingly toward others, the best thing I could do was bless them.

One day when the kids were little, I took a few moments to bless my family one by one at the dinner table, starting with little Abigail. She was so cute sitting there in her high chair—curls of blonde hair dancing around her bright eyes and her two-year-old cheeks smudged with half her dinner.

"Abby," I said with a grin, "I love you, my sweet little girl. I just want you to know that I think you are the cutest, most beautiful little girl in the world."

She stopped squishing her food and looked me deeply in the eye.

"You are so fun and so precious," I continued. "I love you more than the whole wide world."

She was like a little balloon slowly being inflated. You could almost see her tiny spirit growing.

I kept going. "Abby, you're so special, and God is going to do special things in your life."

She couldn't take it anymore—the balloon had to burst. Abruptly, she spun toward my wife, and in her two-year-old English she blurted out, "Mommy, I love you!"

Blessed people bless people.

Researchers A. M. Isen and P. F. Levine conducted a famous study in 1972 that observed the potential altruism of people who have just stepped out of a phone booth (an ancient clear box used for making phone calls for a fee).

On the sidewalk, a seemingly random passerby would drop some papers just as the person stepped out of the phone booth. The question of the study was simple—how many people, after making a phone call, would stoop down and help the poor lady pick up her fumbled papers? The researchers were surprised to discover that only a dismal 4 percent of people helped. But the researchers noticed something that occurred in nearly 100 percent of those studied: they reached into the coin return to check for a possible random coin left behind. So the researchers amended the experiment. They hid a dime in the coin return so that everyone studied found it right before exiting the phone booth.

What researchers observed was astounding: 87 percent of those who had found the surprise dime stooped down to help the lady with the fumbled papers. People were twenty-two times more likely to help someone else if they had found a dime![1]

If people are twenty-two times nicer when they find ten cents in a phone booth, what manner of radical love might fill their hearts if they discovered themselves blessed with every spiritual blessing in Christ?

I think of Zacchaeus, the despised chief tax collector who climbed a sycamore tree to get a glimpse of the famous rabbi visiting Jericho. Jesus pointed to the corrupt tax man, who was despised as a traitor by his fellow Jews, and instead of cursing the greedy little fellow, Jesus blessed him: "Zacchaeus, you're the kind of person I'd like to get to know better. How about having lunch with me?" Jesus gave Zacchaeus no law, no ultimatum. He just blessed the sinner, and Zacchaeus spontaneously decided to give half his wealth to the poor and restore to the people he'd cheated fourfold (Luke 19:1–10).

People don't become more loving, kind, and generous when we tell them they "ought" to be better Christians; people become more loving, kind, and generous when we bless them.

Blessed People Are More Fruitful Than Stressed People

When our son was a teenager, a dear friend and ministry board member, Bob Roach, wanted to invest in Bennett's golf game by purchasing him a new putter.

"Bennett, I'll take you to the golf store and get you that new putter you want. But," Bob added with a wry smile, "you'll have to prove that the new putter works. I want to see you make some six footers on the store's artificial putting green. Make eight out of ten and that putter's yours." We knew he was just joking, since Bob loves Bennett like a grandson. It wasn't the first time he'd invested in Bennett's golf.

The day arrived, and we happily ventured to Golf Galaxy, where Bennett located the precious putter.

"All right," Bob declared, "let's see how well you can putt with it."

Happy and blessed, young Bennett started making six-foot putts without thought. One or two of the balls lipped out, but the boy was sinking most of them with the ease of a vintage Tiger Woods. Then my friend interrupted Bennett's successful run.

"By my count," Bob said with sudden seriousness, "you're seven of nine. You have one putt left. You have to make this one or else."

What? We had thought that the eight-out-of-ten stipulation was a playful joke. But now Bennett's benefactor seemed serious. The requirement wasn't a whimsical ruse—it was a law. Miss the final putt and the putter went back on the shelf.

When Bennett realized the gift was at risk, he did something absurd. He stepped out of the putting stance from which he had made all those putts so easily, stood behind the ball, and studied the line of the putt, as if conditions had mysteriously changed on the green carpet. He hovered nervously over the ball. When he finally stroked the all-important putt, he yanked it left and missed the hole by a mile.

Bennett had made seven putts without a thought. But suddenly, for one key putt, he was at his worst. What changed? The introduction of the law: "If you prove yourself good enough, then you will be blessed."

Years ago, Anne, Abby, and I joined Bennett for a tour of a prospective college. The student tour guide was amiable and instructive, but halfway through the tour she stopped midsentence and pointed at me. "Sir, there is a spider on your collar."

"On *my* collar?" I asked.

"Yes, sir, a big spider on the collar of your shirt."

Have you ever noticed that you can't see your own collar? Was it a tarantula? A black widow? Which collar—right or left? Interestingly, no one made a move to help me. The tour guide, the tour group, and my own family just stared at me, horrified.

That's what the law does—it just tells you about your problem. "Excuse me, sir, but you have a lot of selfishness in your heart. . . . Excuse me, sir, I see some gluttony on your collar."

The law made Bennett think about missing the putt, and the accompanying nervousness took him out of his rhythm. Even PGA pros miss putts when they think about the pressure and get uptight. According to Paul, not only does the law have no power to make us better, but it actually makes us worse: "The law made us want to do sinful things" (Rom. 7:5 NCV).

Many years ago, when my mentor, Dudley Hall, threw a birthday party for his five-year-old son, David, he gathered the boys for some pre-party instructions: "You can climb the trees. You can jump on the trampoline. You can romp with the dogs. . . . But there is just one thing. Do you see that flower bed right over there? No one is to spit in the flower bed. Absolutely no one is to spit in that flower bed."[2] By the end of the party, every boy had spat in the flower bed that they otherwise wouldn't have even noticed.

Of course, the goal of the law (i.e., making the putt) isn't bad. Making the putt is a good thing—it's the desired end. It's not a question of whether it's good to make more putts. It's not a question in life of whether keeping the Ten Commandments is good—of course it's better to be honest, faithful, and upright. But laying down the law bears no fruit. When we're just told about the spider on our collar but given no help, we get anxious, and when no one helps us, we get exhausted in the futile attempt to rid ourselves of our dangerous flaws. The law makes us anxious and exhausted. When we're worried and weary, we're at our worst. Fear makes us choke or panic.

According to Malcolm Gladwell's research, there's a difference between choking and panicking.[3] When we choke, we think too much about the potential negative outcome, we get nervous, and we lose our fluidity and creativity. When we panic, we can't think at all.

Some years ago, our church was frivolously sued, and a bitter lawyer deposed me for three days. On the third day, a second lawyer started deposing me as well. When he asked me the names of the twelve elders I worked with closely day in and day out, I panicked and could only think of one or two names. Have you ever had your brain shut down like that? Fear paralyzes.

If you want someone to choke or panic, keep laying down the law: "You must make the putt or else." If you want someone to be doubly fruitful, speak blessing: "I know you're a good golfer—I bet you can make eight out of ten, so let me see you do it."

Bob *was* joking. He gave Bennett the putter anyway. The next week Bennett played his best competitive golf ever and got his picture in the paper as runner-up in the county junior tournament.

People Work Harder When They Are Blessed

Abby, a junior in college, texted me the other day about an appointment she had with one of her professors. It's a class that requires a verbal presentation every week.

"I went to see him because we've received no grades so far," she said. "It's all being measured by our performance in class, so I wanted to know how I was doing."

"You're doing well," the professor said. "But I don't want to tell you how well because I want you to stay motivated."

Abby texted me a laughing face emoji and said, "Classic case of withholding the blessing, huh, Dad?"

A lot of parents, teachers, coaches, and preachers try to motivate people by withholding their blessing. They're concerned that the affirmation will go to folks' heads and they'll quit trying so hard. They're wrong. Blessed people work harder than those searching for blessing. I saw that in our kids.

Most parents want to motivate their kids to study hard in school. Of course, book learning is not every kid's strength, so don't get uptight if your child isn't at the top of the class. That said, Bennett and Abby are the kind of kids who have a knack for academics, and they've always studied diligently and done well.

Here's what's crazy—we never told the kids to study hard. In fact, I often said the opposite. The following conversation is based on true events.

"Hey, Bennett, it's a nice day. Let's go play some golf."

"I wish I could, Dad, but I've got some AP physics homework to do."

"Aw, come on, Son, it's beautiful outside."

"Wish I could. Gotta study."

Bennett took a bunch of AP classes in high school, earned a biomedical engineering degree in undergraduate school, and is in his third year of law school now. I never once had to crack the whip and say, "You better hit the books." Some of the law exams are eight hours long—I think Bennett sort of likes them.

Abby's been just as hardworking. I especially think of her competitive public speaking career. The national league in which she competed was intense. All speeches had to be memorized and reviewed by officials for proper notation. The competitors had to arrive on-site at 7:00 a.m. in dress clothes for the opening orientation. Tournaments were grueling. By her senior year, Abby was giving five speeches three times a day for four days in front of different judge panels. But we never once had to crack the whip and say, "Abby, you better get to work on your speeches."

If we never pressured or nagged them, where did they get their work ethic?

We celebrated learning, and we blessed them. When Bennett was a preschooler, he wrote a rudimentary "B" in crayon on a piece of paper and brought his accomplishment to his mother. Anne said, "That's so wonderful—you're learning to write. I think you're going to be a good writer and reader." Bennett started dancing around the room, and we joined in. It was the inauguration of a ridiculous tradition we call "family dance." Anyone, at any time, for any reason, can call for a family dance to celebrate a blessing. We close the curtains, turn on lively music, and dance awkwardly.

If learning is a delight instead of a law, kids will want to learn. Kids who think they have academic potential want to study. We told our kids, "God gave you a good brain" so often that they wanted to use it.

The eighteenth-century evangelist John Wesley, known as the father of Methodism, had a legendary work ethic. He traveled thousands of miles by horseback, preached thousands of open-air sermons to masses, and started a global movement of methodical discipleship. Regarding hard work, Wesley wrote, "Never leave anything till tomorrow, which you can do today. And do it as well as possible. Do not sleep or yawn over it: Put your whole strength to work."[4]

Wesley's mother, Susanna, raised her ten children with plenty of love and discipline, but I think John Wesley's work ethic had deeper roots than his well-ordered upbringing. On February 9, 1709, his eleven-year-old sister ran to their father's room because burning pieces of the roof were dropping onto her bed. Flames soon engulfed the house. A servant named Betty ran to the nursery, scooped up the little ones, and told five-year-old John—"Jacky"—to follow her. But when Betty arrived outside at the garden to join the others, young Jacky wasn't with her. When he had seen the flames, he turned back to his room.

Despairing of saving him, John's father knelt with the family outside and prayed for God to receive his little boy's soul. But as they prayed, John cried out from an upstairs window. A quick-thinking neighbor stood on another's shoulders and was able to retrieve the boy a moment before the burning house collapsed. Thereafter Susanna referred to her boy as "a brand plucked from the burning," a reference to Zechariah 3:2. Her blessing went deep into Wesley, who often called himself "a brand plucked from the burning" and once considered it for his epitaph.[5]

If you see yourself as saved for a great purpose, you burn with energy to fulfill your calling.

Blessed People Are Supernaturally Empowered for Fruitfulness

When we bless others to be like Ephraim and Manasseh, we mystically connect their lives to God. Blessing helps people perform better and work harder, but most importantly, blessing helps people trust God and expect His supernatural grace to produce fruit in their lives. Notice again what Joseph said when he named his secondborn Ephraim: "*God* has made me fruitful" (Gen. 41:52, emphasis mine). Joseph's life had been supernaturally, providentially guided and empowered in order to make him doubly fruitful despite all his hardship, and he knew it. Every time Joseph uttered Ephraim's name, he thought of God, the giver of all good gifts.

When we pray for others, we ask God to do wonderful things for them. But when we bless others, we *connect* them to the wonders God has done and is doing.

When you're blessing others, look for ways to help them see their lives like Joseph did—seeing the big, beautiful picture of God's supernatural providence.

After God blessed Jacob amid a dream about a ladder filled with angels, Jacob awoke and declared, "Surely the LORD is in this place and I did not know it" (Gen. 28:16). When you bless people, you are helping them see the places in their lives where the Lord is but they didn't know it.

Well-known author and pastor Tim Keller has comically but poignantly woven together the life events that led him to pastoring Redeemer Church in Manhattan. He and his wife were sent to plant the church. Why were they sent? Because they were in a Presbyterian denomination that emphasized church planting. Why were they Presbyterian? Because in his last year at seminary, Keller took two courses under a particular British professor who convinced him to adopt the beliefs of Presbyterianism. Why was that professor at the seminary? Because, after a long wait, he had acquired a visa to teach in the United States. Why did he finally get the visa (after much trouble)? Because one of the students at the seminary was able to expedite it since, remarkably, he was the son of the sitting president of the United States. Why was his father, Gerald Ford, president? Because Richard

Nixon had resigned. Why had Nixon resigned? Because of the Watergate scandal.

"See," Keller said, "even Watergate is working for you."[6]

In the end, Joseph's life was doubly fruitful in Egypt because God was graciously, sovereignly at work bringing all the circumstances together for Joseph's good and for the salvation of the world. When you bless someone to be like Ephraim, you're invoking the name "twice fruitful," knowing that God can do "far more than you could ever imagine or guess or request in your wildest dreams" (Eph. 3:20 Message).

7

Blessed to Be Favored

Our children never resented being the preacher's kids. They loved it. I'd heard all the nightmare stories about PKs going wild in resentment of the church, so whenever Anne brought two-year-old Bennett by my office, I'd give him a pencil or other trinket and say, "Hey, Bennett, you know why you're getting that pencil? You're the pastor's son. You're favored."

When we'd take the kids to Chuck E. Cheese on a Monday because that was my only day off, I'd say, "Hey, Bennett and Abby, isn't this cool? We can play whatever games we want because hardly anyone is here. You know why you get to be here on a Monday? Because you're the pastor's kids." We never highlighted all the stuff we *couldn't* do on a Saturday or Sunday.

Sometimes I'd have a really big example, like the time a parishioner gave us the cruise she was awarded when she bought a timeshare. Every time we snorkeled or feasted or roamed the ship, I'd say, "You know why you get to do this, right?" By the time they were teenagers they liked going to church more than I did.

Life's a matter of perspective. If you live under the law, you get in a bad mood if your hard work isn't rewarded to your satisfaction. But when you live in grace, you rejoice over every good gift because you know it was never guaranteed and you didn't deserve it.

So we blessed the kids every day using the words of Luke 2:52: "May you grow in wisdom, stature, and favor with God and people all your life." I wanted them to know that the favor of God is to be treasured more than skill and intelligence. I wanted them to know the favor of God not just so they would have doors miraculously open for them but also because I wanted them to see themselves in the light of grace. When we know we have the favor of God on our lives, we become expectant, grateful, and joyful.

God's favor can do for us what we could never accomplish on our own. Unmerited favor is the heart of all blessing and is the climax of the wondrous Ephraim and Manasseh story.

When Jacob crossed his arms, deliberately placing his right hand on the undeserving younger child, the patriarch was announcing, "Unmerited favor be upon you." His crossed arms revealed that the old, conniving workhorse of a man finally had seen into the riches of God's free grace. To say, "May God make you as Ephraim and Manasseh" is to say, "May your life be fueled by grace and filled with blessing beyond your deserving because you are highly favored."

Apples to Apples

Stanley Bennett is laughing, playing the harmonica, and telling stories in heaven now, but he had plenty of practice on earth. My wife's uncle Stanley was a round-faced, bald Presbyterian minister who laughed as easily as a toddler and counseled as wisely as Solomon. For decades, we'd load up the car, drive to Stanley and Joella's home in the North Carolina mountains, and talk about ministry, Jesus, and life. Stanley's adventurous ministry career included stuff like planting a church, leading a college campus ministry, spending eight years flying solo evangelistic missions into the Brazilian jungle, and serving in a Los Angeles mega-church. But it wasn't his fascinating ministry experience that I loved most—it was his understanding of grace that he'd discovered as a boy.

Stanley, the sixth of eight children in York, South Carolina, got bored and hungry one day, so he and his brother Douglas ("Duddy") snuck into the neighbor's yard to steal apples. They thought they had skulked into the yard undetected, but Mrs. Correll saw the whole thing.

"Boys, I see you there. You two come in here this instant!"

They'd been caught red-handed with her green apples. Tails between their legs, Stanley and Duddy slumped into Mrs. Correll's house with red faces.

"Boys, you just sit right here," she said, directing them to two dining room chairs. "I'll be back in a moment."

Stanley knew what she must be doing. Surely she was calling his father, who was the chief of police in York and tolerated no mischief. Stanley knew that his face wasn't the only thing that was going to be red that day.

Instead, Mrs. Correll emerged from the pantry with a bowl of the biggest, reddest, shiniest apples Stanley and his brother had ever seen. "Boys, those green apples on my tree are sour and wormy. They aren't any good. Here, try these."

For a long time Stanley and Duddy just sat there looking at the bright apples. Stanley had never eaten a store-bought apple. He couldn't believe his eyes.

Grace isn't grace unless it seems too good to be true. If you don't wonder a little if something is a cruel trick or a clever ruse, you probably aren't encountering the unmerited favor of God.

Finally, Stanley took a bite. It was the best apple he'd ever tasted. After a hesitant start, he finally chomped down the gift and just let the juice splatter where it may.

"Now, boys, I don't ever want to see you eating those bitter green apples in my backyard. I always have good store-bought apples in my kitchen, and I'd like you to come over any time you're hungry," Mrs. Correll said.

Stanley looked up and saw himself in Mrs. Correll's big, wood-framed mirror.

"I stared at my reflection in that mirror," he told me. "I should have been getting ready for a spanking from my dad, but instead, I saw myself in that mirror with juice running down my chin. That's the day I discovered the meaning of grace."

Jacob Finally Grasps Grace

Old man Jacob's life was woven with worry, soaked in struggle, and seared with grief. When you consider a litany of his strife, pain, and deceit, it's backbreaking:

- He struggled in the womb with his twin brother (Gen. 25:22).
- Born second, he came into the world grabbing his brother's heel (25:26).
- His father loved Esau more than him (25:28).
- He leveraged Esau's momentary hunger and bought his brother's birthright with a pot of stew (25:33).
- He pretended to be Esau, duped his father, and stole the special patriarchal blessing that was supposed to be spoken over the firstborn (27:1–41).
- He fled for fear of his embittered brother's murderous intent (28:10).
- He worked seven years in order to marry Rachel, was tricked, and had to work seven more years for his father-in-law, Laban (29:18–30).
- Jacob's wives and maidservants filled his home with strife as they competed to bear children (29:16–30:24).
- He duped Laban in a business deal by crossbreeding the sheep and got rich by his trickery (30:25–43).
- He wrestled all night long with a messenger of God (32:22–32).
- His daughter was raped by a foreigner (34:2).
- His beloved wife Rachel died in childbirth (35:16–20).
- His sons hated Joseph because he was Jacob's favorite, so they sold him into slavery and led their father to believe that his beloved Joseph was dead (37:1–36).
- He grieved for decades a loss that was a lie, not knowing that Joseph was alive, ruling, and prospering in Egypt (42:38).

Jacob struggled his whole life to earn what can only be given. He had the favor of God on his life and didn't know it.

Jacob was blind to grace. How ironic. He spent decades grieving how unblessed he was for the loss of Joseph, and all the while, Joseph was ruling in Egypt. When Jacob's sons told him that Joseph was alive, "his heart became numb, for he did not believe them" (45:26). When aged Jacob was reunited with his son, Joseph "wept on his neck a good while" (46:29).

When Jacob drew near to death, Joseph rushed his boys to their grandfather's bedside. "Israel said to Joseph, 'I never expected to see your face; and behold, God has let me see your offspring also'" (48:11).

"I never expected . . . and behold, God has let . . ."

Suddenly, grace broke through.

The way Jacob a moment later referenced God in his blessing proved that he suddenly saw his life differently: "The God who has been my shepherd all my life long" (48:15).

There was something about seeing his grandchildren that made Jacob reinterpret his whole history. What had his perpetual struggle for first place gotten him? Nothing but weariness and grief.

But there on his deathbed, seeing the precious grandsons he could have never imagined, Jacob discovered the unquenchable kindness of God. It finally dawned on him: God had been there all his life long. Jacob hadn't been cursed for being the secondborn. He was blessed. He hadn't been overlooked by God. He was favored.

So Jacob lifted his right hand of stronger blessing from the head of the entitled firstborn, Manasseh, and placed it on the younger son, Ephraim, who didn't deserve it in the least. Joseph tried to correct him, saying, "Not this way, my father; since this one is the firstborn, put your right hand on his head" (48:18). But Jacob insisted, "I know, my son, I know" (v. 19). In other words, "I know what you're saying, Joseph. I know the custom dictates that the firstborn gets the stronger blessing. I know I am supposed to put my right hand on the older. I know all that, but trust me, I know what I'm doing. For once in my long, struggle-filled life, I'm not confused. I'm more clear-minded now than I've ever been in my life. Let me cross my arms and put Ephraim first. Let my final act be one of grace."

So Jacob showed Ephraim unmerited favor and announced, "By you Israel will pronounce blessings, saying 'God make you as Ephraim and Manasseh'" (48:20). Jacob saw in the Spirit the blessing God wants spoken over every child of God: "May your life be shaped not by your strife-filled effort but by the grace of God. May all your days be filled with the expectancy, joy, and gratitude that comes when you have been shown unmerited favor."

Oh, to Be a Firstborn

I'm the third of three boys. My oldest brother was a star student and athlete and, well, the star of everything. Remember that prestigious Morehead Scholarship that Mickey Thigpen unexpectedly received? Well, my big brother got one too, but no one was surprised. As commonly reported, firstborns are more likely to be leaders. They are 30 percent more likely to be CEOs than non-firstborns.

Well, of course.

I was at the beach one summer reading a book when I couldn't help but notice the red-haired cutie who kept toddling to and from the surf with her little bucket. I think she was two. Underneath four umbrellas sat about twelve family members—presumably parents, grandparents, aunts, and uncles. The red-haired darling was clearly the only child. I looked up from my book and chuckled. Here was a two-year-old who was the center of attention of twelve doting adults, who were there to affirm to her that she was, undoubtedly, the cutest and smartest little girl ever born.

She'll probably grow up to run a company—or the country.

My oldest brother excelled early in academics. Of course he did. Everybody read to him for hours every day. By the time I came along, the books were lost or chewed up, and everyone was too tired to read to anybody. I say it with a grin, but we thirdborns know it's true. All the attention goes to the favored firstborns, and the rest of us just fend for ourselves.

If firstborns garner more attention in American culture, imagine the favor they received in ancient Middle Eastern society. The weight of the family legacy rested upon the firstborn son. He would carry on the family business, manage the family estate, and care for his widowed mother. So as was fitting, he received not only the adulation of society but also a double portion of his father's inheritance. When the firstborn son was welcomed into the world, the whole village celebrated. Who wouldn't want to be the firstborn son?

It was as if Jacob knew all about the firstborn's privileges as he grasped his brother's foot at birth. Esau won the race into the world, with Jacob yanking on his heel as if to say, "No, no! I want to be in first place." Years later, when Jacob pretended to be Esau and duped Isaac into blessing him, the bereft older sibling desperately begged for his daddy's blessing: "He cried out with an exceedingly great and bitter cry and said to his father, 'Bless me, even me also, O my father!'" (Gen. 27:34). But there was no redo. Jacob had stolen the blessing and Esau was left weeping and pleading, "Have you but one blessing, my father? Bless me, even me also, O my father" (v. 38).

Esau's mourning cry haunts me because it's the same silent wail that was buried in my own heart when I asked my father to bless me in the counselor's office. It's the hidden cry of countless sons and daughters everywhere: *Daddy, where's my blessing? Daddy, will you please bless me? I feel so alone, so overlooked. Oh, Daddy, bless me!*

If you bristle at the unfairness of the older Esau being overlooked while the conniving scoundrel Jacob was blessed, good. You're on the rim of the Grand Canyon getting ready to see the most majestic wonder of the gospel. If you're bothered that Jacob deliberately crossed his arms and blessed the wrong child, excellent. You're ready to behold the most unfair, most glorious gift of the Ephraim and Manasseh blessing.

The Day God Crossed His Arms

Jacob's blessing of Ephraim and Manasseh was a shadow, a prefiguring, of the day God would cross His arms in the heavenlies. Fifth-century church father Saint Augustine wrote, "In the Old Testament the New is concealed, in the New the Old is revealed."[1] He was describing what Paul meant in reference to the Old Testament images of festivals, ceremonial laws, and Sabbaths: "These are a shadow of the things to come, but the substance belongs to Christ" (Col. 2:17).

Similarly, the writer of Hebrews referred to the law as "a shadow of the good things to come instead of the true form of these realities" (Heb. 10:1). God made it His mysterious habit to orchestrate real-life events in the Old Testament story that point to the ultimate story of Jesus. If you see a shadow of a person, you know that the person must exist, but until you see their face in broad daylight, you've not seen the real thing. For example, the lamb that every Hebrew family sacrificed every Passover for centuries was only a shadow of the "Lamb of God, who takes away the sin of the world" (John 1:29). God was filling history with the foreshadowing of His Son. So the Spirit inspired Jacob to cross his arms from his deathbed because God would one day cross His arms to give us life.

In the fullness of time, God sent His firstborn Son into a woefully broken world. Jesus, "the firstborn of all creation" (Col. 1:15), lived a sinless life. He loved perfectly. He healed the sick, fed the poor, and taught the truth. He was the noble, firstborn Son who deserved only His Father's strong right hand of blessing.

But He was reviled and hated by those He came to save, and by God's set purpose, Jesus was nailed to a Roman cross. There, as He slowly suffocated to death, "Jesus cried out with a loud voice, saying, 'Eli, Eli, lema sabachthani?' that is, 'My God, my God, why have you forsaken me?'" (Matt. 27:46).

He might as well have cried, "Father, where is your right hand of blessing? Daddy, where's my blessing?"

Jesus cried out in desolation because His Father did the unthinkable. God crossed His arms. He lifted His strong right hand from the firstborn's bleeding head and stretched it toward the head of the undeserving secondborn—you and me.

While God's firstborn hung on the cross, He redeemed us from the curse of the law by becoming a curse for us (Gal. 3:13), while the Father's right hand of blessing came to rest upon you and me and anyone who trusts in Christ.

If you are a Christian, God has made you like Ephraim and Manasseh: He has made you a child of grace. He has made you a picture of unmerited favor. Though it bends the mind to consider it, you've received the blessing that should have rested solely on Jesus.

Such a soaring thought stretches the imagination but is, in the end, the only way to comprehend the words of Paul: "Blessed be the God and Father of our Lord Jesus Christ, who has blessed us in Christ with every spiritual blessing in the heavenly places" (Eph. 1:3).

To be a Christian means that Christ exchanged places with us. "For our sake he made him to be sin who knew no sin, so that in him we might become the righteousness of God" (2 Cor. 5:21). This means that Jesus took our every sin and gave to us His own blessing. It means that because he stood in our place, you and I are privileged to stand in His place. It means that the Father loves us in the same manner and to the same infinite degree that He loves His only begotten Son. It means that God blesses every believer with Jesus's own inheritance.

His joy, His life, His eternal happiness become yours. Christians have become "heirs of God and fellow heirs with

Christ" (Rom. 8:17). We have been "raised . . . up with him and seated . . . with him in the heavenly places" (Eph. 2:6).

The Father has crossed His arms. Maybe the angels tried to stop Him, but He could not be restrained. He is God Almighty and He knew what He was doing.

In Christ, you have been made as Ephraim and Manasseh.

The Power of Favor

In 1981, the Chapel Hill basketball arena, which normally spilled over with fans watching Michael Jordan fly to the rim, was filled with students listening to the world's most famous evangelist. Billy Graham had come to the University of North Carolina to give a series of lectures. Thousands of students indicated decisions for Christ that week. Some friends and I started a Bible study in our dorm for some of the new Christians.

The first time I heard Billy Graham in person, I was enthralled. But when other students asked me what was so riveting about his messages, I couldn't give a good answer. Graham didn't rise to prominence because he was the greatest expositor of Scripture or the most eloquent orator. The first sermons he preached were ones he'd memorized from a book. Sure, there was something magnetic about the wiry, wavy-haired North Carolina farm boy, but what catapulted him onto the international platform?

The 1949 Los Angeles revival was key. In his autobiography, Graham summed up his watershed meetings' success as entirely "*God's* doing" (emphasis his). The revival actually got off to a slow start. The tent seated six thousand, but only two to three thousand were attending each night.

Graham's team was praying about whether to extend the revival or shut it down when three momentous things happened. First, a spell of warm weather rolled in on October 17, the day the revival was scheduled to close. Second, a well-known country singer named Stew Hamblen accepted Christ after meeting with Billy at a hotel. After Hamblen professed his faith publicly at the crusade, crowds began to swell. Third and most important, though the local press had paid little attention initially to the meetings, one night Graham found the tent swarming with reporters, flash-bulbs popping, and journalists scribbling notes.

One of the reporters told Billy Graham, "You have been kissed by William Randolph Hearst." The publishing mogul had, for a still unknown reason, directed his newspapers to give extra attention to the revival meetings. Rumors reported that Hearst distributed a memo reading simply, "Puff Graham."[2]

Billy Graham didn't become the twentieth century's most influential spiritual leader because he was the best preacher. It was the favor of God. When you live by the favor of God rather than personal ambition, anything can happen.

Joseph, while incarcerated, was given "favor in the sight of the keeper of the prison" (Gen. 39:21). In the Exodus story, the fleeing, freshly emancipated Hebrew slaves collected gold and jewelry from their captors because "the LORD had given the people favor in the sight of the Egyptians" (Exod. 12:36). David survived King Saul's murderous threats because he had found favor with the king's son (1 Sam. 20:3). Nehemiah led the successful Jerusalem wall restoration project because he had asked God for favor with the king (Neh. 1:11). Esther became the heroic queen who saved her people because when she met the king, she "won his favor" (Esther 2:9). Though Daniel was an exile in Babylon, "God gave [him] favor . . . in the sight of the chief" (Dan. 1:9). Mary became the mother of the Messiah because the Nazarene peasant girl had "found favor with God" (Luke 1:30). Jesus Himself grew in favor with God and people (Luke 2:52).

If you want to change the world, bless someone to walk in the favor of God. If you want others to be used of God beyond imagination, bless them to be as Ephraim and Manasseh because it's a picture of unmerited favor. It's a picture of the gospel.

Uncle Stanley had an interesting ministry assignment that I didn't mention earlier. He served for years as the pastor of the Montreat Presbyterian Church in the North Carolina mountains, where the Grahams were members. Stanley was Billy Graham's pastor. Sometimes Billy would fill the pulpit when Stanley was away. Stanley laughed when he told me, "I could preach till I was blue in the face and not get a soul to make a decision for Christ, but Billy would cough and the whole church would come forward."

I have a letter that Billy Graham sent to Stanley after preaching in his church one Sunday. "I enjoyed preaching in your pulpit this past Sunday," he wrote. "I am afraid, however, I did a very poor job. One of my little girls remarked, 'I like Uncle Stanley's better.'"

After the day Mrs. Correll caught Stanley stealing apples, he never stole anything again. Unmerited favor will do that to you. When Mrs. Correll grew old and planned to sell her house in York in order to move into a retirement facility, she called the Bennett children and asked them to choose whatever furniture of hers they might want. Stanley took only one item—the big, wood-framed mirror that hung in the dining room.

Once you've looked grace in the face, you never want to forget it.

Spend time every day thinking about the grace of God. Write down your God moments of unmerited favor.

Better yet, find a mirror, cross your arms, and say, "Thank you, God, for making me like Ephraim and Manasseh."

PART THREE

GIVING
the BLESSING

8

Why Blessing Works

I finally figured out my job. I'm a color commentator for Jesus.

While a 350-pound football player sweats on the turf, the TV color commentator sits in the air-conditioned box wearing headphones and drawing yellow Telestrator lines on the screen. He draws a circle and says, "Watch in slow motion how the right tackle blocks the blitzing linebacker." Then the commentator draws a yellow arrow and says, "Look at this huge hole in the line that the tailback ran through. That's how they scored—it was because of the right tackle's great block." And if you're a sports fan, you say to yourself, *Wow, I didn't notice him making that great block. I was focused on the running back.*

I like the color commentary because it helps me appreciate what the athletes are doing. I like knowing how things work. So I'd like to offer a little color commentary in order to show how blessing works.

When we watch the slow-motion replay of blessing in action, we'll see three powerful biblical principles converge. Blessing works because of the power of faith, the power of words, and the power of sowing and reaping.

The Power of Faith

How Jacob Made the Hall of Fame

The eleventh chapter of Hebrews is a sort of Hall of Fame for the biblical characters who had the greatest faith. The litany of faith heroes starts with God Himself, who modeled perfect faith in creating the cosmos from nothing (Heb. 11:3). The remainder of the chapter highlights an impressive list of people who had mountain-moving faith. Mostly, it's the Bible greats you'd expect:

- Noah built a huge boat on dry ground because he had faith that the rain was coming, though there wasn't a cloud in the sky.
- Abraham and Sarah, the hundred-year-old man and his ninety-year-old wife, believed they were going to have a baby who would be the seed of a nation.
- Joshua marched around the thick walls of Jericho because he believed they would tumble at the sound of the trumpet.

This faith Hall of Fame list also includes Moses, Daniel, David, Samson, and the great prophets. There are no surprises there, except one: "By faith Jacob, when dying, blessed each of the sons of Joseph, bowing in worship over the head of his staff" (v. 21).

Old Jacob made the list? The conniving, confused deceiver found a place next to Samson and Moses and David? An old man leaning on his staff and speaking blessing made the famous Hebrews 11 chapter? Is blessing someone an act of faith on par with the Red Sea parting and Jericho walls tumbling?

Absolutely.

In God's eyes, blessing others is one of the most powerful expressions of faith on earth. If you can envision a positive future for someone and speak it out in faith, you're in God's faith Hall of Fame.

Blessing always begins with your faith for others to flourish. When Jacob blessed his sons, he pictured rulership for Judah: "Your brothers shall praise you; your hand shall be on the neck of your enemies" (Gen. 49:8). When he blessed Joseph, Jacob envisioned abundant fruit: "Joseph is a fruitful bough, a fruitful bough by a spring; his branches run over the wall" (v. 22). Gary Smalley and John Trent call this element of blessing "picturing a special future."[1] In other words, faith has spiritual eyes to see what can be. I think of faith as a sanctified imagination.

Sanctified Imagination

Imagination is a uniquely human faculty. Only humans can deliberately envision complex future realities that do not yet exist. When the Wright brothers flew their first manned flights of a few hundred feet at Kitty Hawk, it wasn't the chilly December beach winds that lifted them as much as it was their imagination. It isn't Cinderella's castle or Space Mountain that has made Disney World the most visited resort in the world. It was Walt's imagination that led him to buy the thirty thousand acres of central Florida swamp and cattle land as he dreamed of creating the "happiest place on earth."

Only a human being can stand in front of 250,000 civil rights supporters on a hot August 1963 day in the midst of national, social inequality and declare, "I have a dream that my four little children will one day live in a nation where they will not be judged by the color of their skin but by the content of their character."[2] Only humans imagine new societies.

It's godlike to imagine something new.

God's Word is replete with images, stories, and metaphors designed to ignite our imagination. The Lord spoke through Jeremiah so we could imagine Him as a potter remolding clay. He spoke through Isaiah so we could see ourselves mounting up with wings as eagles. He gave Daniel a dream interpretation so we could imagine Christ's reign crushing every other kingdom. Jesus appealed to listeners' imaginations in almost every teaching: "Imagine a mountain being thrown into the sea. . . . Imagine a Father who had two sons. . . . Imagine a king who threw a great party." Ultimately, God wants us to imagine having a new, spiritual body and living forever in a new heaven and a new earth.

So if you want to bless someone, use your imagination. Think of someone you love—what can you imagine God doing in their life? Open your eyes of faith—envision someone in the fullness of the Ephraim and Manasseh blessing.

Use your imagination to see God cross His arms, placing the right hand of unmerited favor on the head of your loved one. What spiritual riches do you see?

Faith Is Contagious

People don't need your advice as much as they need your faith. Blessing is powerful because it doesn't tell people that they *ought to have* more faith—blessing *gives* them faith.

Years ago, the Weather Channel produced a realistic, dramatic reenactment of a stirring rescue. A rising flood was quickly filling a highway tunnel. Most of the cars had escaped the tunnel, but one driver was trapped. Hysterical, the stranded woman had climbed on top of her car. As the water rose higher, so did her screams for help. Providentially, there was one other driver in the tunnel. He was an off-duty firefighter who was also a trained lifeguard. As the heroic rescuer began swimming toward the panic-stricken woman, he called out, "You are not going to die today!"

The woman's desperate cries softened.

The rescuer knew that the greatest danger to a drowning person is panic. A panicked person might scratch, claw, or immobilize the rescuer. So the firefighter cried out again, "You are not going to die today!"

Her hysteria calmed enough for the firefighter to secure her and swim outside the tunnel. Though she didn't have faith for escape, the rescuer did. She didn't need a swimming lesson, and she didn't need him to yell, "Calm down, woman!" She didn't need his advice. She needed his faith.

When you bless others, you build their faith by lighting up their imaginations. Jacob had a vision of what Ephraim and Manasseh could be by God's grace. Though he was old and his eyesight was dim, his spiritual vision had never been sharper. Later, when he put his hands on his twelve sons and blessed their future, it earned him a spot in the Hebrews 11 Hall of Fame because the men believed Jacob's vision for their lives.

You don't ever need to struggle to imagine a positive vision for someone's life because you can always announce what the Bible has to say about them. The highest and best expressions of faith are rooted in the original source of faith—the Word of God. "Faith comes from hearing, and hearing through the word of Christ" (Rom. 10:17). God's Word is an expression of God's faith for you. When you read it, you are aligning yourself with what God believes and says. When you bless others in accord with God's Word, you're affirming the vision God has for them. As we learned from John Calvin, the Scriptures are like eyeglasses. We don't just look *at* the Word of God—we look at all of life *through* the Word of God. God wants you to see your life and others through His Word.

If you sanctify your imagination by aligning it with the Word of God, you'll be filled with faith to bless your own life and the lives of others.

The Power of Words

What the Word Says about Words

What if I told you that you've been given a bag of tools more valuable than any amount of silver or gold? What if I could convince you that your special tools can calm an angry person, heal a wounded soul, fix a broken relationship, help you prosper financially, and determine life and death?

The book of Proverbs has all that and much more to say about the power of words:

> A word fitly spoken
> is like apples of gold in a setting of silver. (25:11)

> A soft answer turns away wrath,
> but a harsh word stirs up anger. (15:1)

> Gracious words are like a honeycomb,
> sweetness to the soul and health to the body.
> (16:24)

> From the fruit of a man's mouth his stomach is
> satisfied;
> he is satisfied by the yield of his lips. (18:20)

> Death and life are in the power of the tongue,
> and those who love it will eat its fruits. (18:21)

In the beginning, as the Spirit of God brooded over the face of the deep, the Lord created the cosmos by speaking. When He said, "Let there be light," energy burst forth because God's spoken word was filled with God Himself. Put this book down for a moment, place the back of your hand an inch from your mouth, and say, "Let there be light." When you said those words, what did you feel on your hand? You felt air from your lungs as you spoke because your words are full of your breath.

In both the Old Testament and the New Testament, the words for breath can also be translated "wind" or "spirit." The Spirit of God infuses the Word of God the way breath fills speech. That's why Paul declared that all Scripture is "God-breathed" (2 Tim. 3:16 NIV). God's Word is full of God, and in a sense, your words are full of you. That's what Jesus implied when He said, "Out of the abundance of the heart [one's] mouth speaks" (Luke 6:45).

The Weight of Our Words

Like imagination, language is God's unique gift to those made in His own image. Stanford University professor Lera Boroditsky has asserted, "Language is a uniquely human gift. When we study language, we are uncovering in part what makes us human, getting a peek at the very nature of human nature."[3]

Without capacity for language, we are less than human. Blind, deaf, and mute, Helen Keller explained that she didn't experience real humanity until she discovered speech. "For nearly six years," she said, "I had no concept of nature or mind or death or God. I literally thought with my body. . . . Then, suddenly . . . I awoke to language, to knowledge of love, to the usual concepts of nature, of good and evil! I was actually lifted from nothingness to human life."[4]

To say that language makes us human is also to say that language makes us godlike. God created the world with words and then gave us words so we can shape the world. James compared the tongue to the rudder that steers a massive ship. A spoken blessing is powerful because words steer others' lives. Change your words, change your world.

Because the Hebrew people understood the creative force of speech in creation, they never treated words as if they could fall empty to the ground. Words, once spoken, are like toothpaste out of the tube—you can't stuff it back in. When Isaac accidentally blessed Jacob rather than Esau, he couldn't retract his words any more than a groom could retract his "I do" the week after his wedding. Words are symbols that carry the full weight of the reality they describe.

When we bless someone, our words convey the blessing. Our blessing doesn't merely reflect someone's value—it bestows worth. If an art expert looks at a painting and declares, "It is a masterpiece," then it is, indeed, a masterpiece.

A twenty-four-year-old Wisconsin man, Manuel Franco, bought $10 worth of Powerball tickets and soon discovered that one of his tickets had won $768 million. He said he couldn't function at work the next day because he was too worried about the ticket being lost or stolen.[5]

On the one hand, the winning lottery ticket was a worthless piece of paper. It was just a symbol. In and of itself, the little piece of paper was worth nothing. On the other hand, this lottery ticket was worth $768 million because the ticket represented the reality. The reality ($768 million of winnings) was so closely linked to the piece of paper that we could say the symbol (the little piece of paper) was indeed worth $768 million. Our words are symbols, but they are symbols so closely aligned with the reality that we can hardly separate the two.

Name-Calling

When my nephew Christopher was a preschooler, one of his aunts asked him what his father and two uncles did. His response was classic: "Daddy is an officer. Uncle Mark shoots big animals. And Uncle Alan tells people about Jesus." He got it more right than meets the eye. His father, my brother David, is a lawyer who works in an office. He thinks, writes, and talks on the phone in his office, so he's an "officer." My brother Mark loves to hunt. In fact, he has always been an adventurer looking for something to conquer—he "shoots big animals." And I . . . well, I am a color commentator for God—I tell people about Jesus.

Isn't it fascinating that even a little child has an instinctive capacity to call things what they are? If Johnny calls Billy "stupid," Billy is likely to shout, "Am not!" because kids scuffling on the school playground know that there's a lot at stake in name-calling. Our words matter so much that society is quicker to tolerate a public business failure or celebrity extramarital affair than it is to overlook any form of prejudicial speech. You can make a lot of errors and keep your job, but if you use the wrong words publicly, you'll be fired. All people, Christian or not, seem to know that it's hellish to call someone by the wrong name.

In the second chapter of Genesis, God brought the animals one by one before Adam "to see what he would call them" (v. 19). God trusted Adam to name the animals properly. Dudley Hall has observed that, before they fell into sin, Adam and Eve knew what to call the animals.[6] Adam didn't call a pig his wife or an ostrich his helpmate. But after sin entered the world, people became confused and called things what they aren't. Eventually, the human ability to properly name things became so corrupted that people began to "call evil good and good evil" (Isa. 5:20).

The forces of hell want us to call people by the wrong name. If we call a smart kid "dumb" long enough, the kid will probably start underachieving. But Jesus, who never mislabeled anyone, came to restore our ability to rightly name things.

A dear parishioner had been hospitalized for the third or fourth time in a battle against cancer (a battle that he's winning as I write). If you've ever been through repeated hospitalizations, you know what it takes out of you. Sometimes you feel like someone has moved the finish line on you. When you think you've finished your treatments, another spot shows up on the scan and you find yourself with another hospital stay. It was one of those times for my parishioner, and it especially had taken a toll on his precious wife of fifty-plus years.

I called the hospital room one day, and his wife answered the phone.

"Greetings, woman of faith and power," I said.

She wept.

She wept with hope and joy and for the reminder that she wasn't a defeated foe. She later told me that my simple greeting sustained her during those difficult days.

"I just needed to be reminded who I am in Christ," she said.

I wasn't making it up. She *is* a woman of great faith and spiritual power. The adversity she and her husband faced didn't define her. The fact that she felt so disappointed and weak didn't change her real identity. To have called her a defeated, faithless doubter would have been as wrong as Adam calling a mouse his helpmate.

When we bless others, we don't fabricate a new identity for them—we confirm their true identity. In Christ, God has restored our capacity to name "the animals."

The Power of Sowing and Reaping

Everything Reproduces after Its Own Kind

A parishioner and dear friend, Tom Wolff, is an internal medicine physician who likes mission trips. Though he's one of the most respected doctors in town, he's a quiet, humble man who'd rather catch a trout than others' praise. But when he came back from a Honduran mission trip some years ago, Tom couldn't wait to tell me about his Rockport shoes.

After caring for hundreds of poor Hondurans who had no other medical care, Tom treated a man who had no shoes. Before releasing the patient, God impressed something on Tom's heart: *Give him your new Rockport shoes.* Tom really liked the Rockports he'd just bought, but he followed the Lord's prompting.

The following week, one of our parishioners, Ralph Hicks, had an appointment with Tom. Ralph was a smart, gracious man skilled in architectural design who suffered from a rare blood disease that eventually took his life. Even while he was sick, he loved giving to others.

"I have something for you," Ralph said at the beginning of their appointment. "I ordered these shoes and they don't fit. They're brand-new, and for some reason, I thought they might fit you."

Ralph handed Tom a box containing the exact style and size of Rockports that the doctor had given to the Honduran man the week before. Of course, Tom could have afforded to buy himself another pair of shoes, but I think the Lord was giving him a wink as He reminded us all about the principle of sowing and reaping.

Blessing is like sowing seed. Every word we speak is like a seed looking for soil in which to germinate. Everything in God's world depends on the rhythm of sowing and reaping. Seed goes into the ground, germinates, sprouts, grows, and bears fruit.

It's good that everything reproduces according to its own kind because we're never left guessing what will come from the seed we sow. "The earth brought forth vegetation, plants yielding seed according to their own kinds, and trees bearing fruit in which is their seed, each according to its kind. And God saw that it was good" (Gen. 1:12). Orange seeds produce orange trees. Apple seeds produce apple trees. Nowhere in nature is the sowing-and-reaping principle violated. You'll never plant an orange seed and get an apple tree. And if that's true in natural things, it's also true in spiritual things. When Paul warns, "Do not be deceived: God is not mocked, for whatever one sows, that will he also reap" (Gal. 6:7), he's affirming the comprehensive force of sowing and reaping.

If a farmer intentionally sows corn kernels because he has a vision of a cornfield, how much more intentional should you be about the spiritual seeds you sow? If you want someone to live a blessed life, sow blessing. If you want an enemy to treat you better, sow seeds of kindness. If you want your struggling student to study more, call him smart. If you want your husband to talk more, tell him how important his thoughts are.

Only the most foolish farmer would sow what he doesn't want to reap. Blessing works because we reap what we sow.

Big Things Start Small

Jesus compared the kingdom of heaven to a mustard seed: "It is the smallest of all seeds, but when it has grown it is larger than all the garden plants and becomes a tree, so that the birds of the air come and make nests in its branches" (Matt. 13:32). Once, while I was preaching on that text, we handed out mustard seeds to each worshiper. I'm sure there are still hundreds of them hidden under pew cushions and in the corners of corridors, because if you drop a mustard seed, you'll never find it. It's almost too small to see. But inside that tiny seed is the whole life of the future mustard plant. A little acorn can produce a towering oak.

The seed principle means we must never underestimate the power of blessing.

The Nobel committee gave the 2019 physiology award to three scientists for discovering how human cells sense and react to low oxygen levels. Their discovery might lead to new treatments for cancer.

One of the winners, Gregg Semenza, at his news conference at Johns Hopkins University School of Medicine, paid tribute to Rose Nelson, his biology teacher at Sleepy Hollow High School in Sleepy Hollow, New York. "She used to say, 'Now when you win your Nobel Prize, I don't want you to forget that you learned that here.'" The esteemed scientist grieved that Rose wasn't alive to see him receive the award. "She was my inspiration," Semenza said.[7]

Don't ever deem your blessing too small to impact a life. Little seeds sown in Sleepy Hollow can grow into towering Nobel Prize–sized oak trees.

Seedtime and Harvest

Don't fret if it seems like your blessing isn't working immediately. Seeds take time to grow. When Mrs. Harper told Mickey Thigpen that she believed he'd be a Morehead Scholar, it was three years before the ninth grader would even have a shot at it. When Julia Mancuso drew a picture of herself winning an Olympic medal, she had to wait nearly a decade to try out for the Olympics. North Carolina farmers don't stress out when nothing is growing in the frigid ground of winter—watermelon isn't supposed to grow in January. Farmers don't panic when corn isn't tasseling in mid-May—the Silver Queen will be sweet by July. "While the earth remains, seedtime and harvest, cold and heat, summer and winter, day and night, shall not cease" (Gen. 8:22).

Blessing, like seed, takes time to sprout, but you don't need the harvest in hand to know that you're blessed. If a farmer has one thousand fertile acres that have been sown with expensive seed, his wealth is real even though it's not yet harvested. You don't have to wait until harvesttime to consider yourself blessed.

As we go deeper into the dynamics of blessing, let's start by learning to bless the person you might neglect most—yourself.

9

Blessing Your Own Life

We were on the way to the golf course when little Bennett blurted out, "Dad, how can you get addicted to something?"

Gulp. He was in fourth grade, and he was already asking me about addiction?

"Well, um . . ." I swallowed hard. "Bennett, if you're addicted to something, you feel like you have to have it, and if you don't have it you start wanting it really bad. Addictions are awful because they take control of your life, and the things you are addicted to usually end up hurting you. Why do you ask?"

"I saw on ESPN something about a professional golfer who blew two million dollars gambling. They said he had a gambling addiction. Can you be addicted to gambling?"

"Yes, you can be addicted to gambling. You can be addicted to a lot of things."

"I don't understand," Bennett mused. "He is famous. He is rich. He gets to play golf all the time and gets paid to do commercials. He has just about the perfect life. Why would he get addicted to something like gambling?"

How could I formulate a ten-year-old version of all that I've learned about the deep, complex sources of addiction? How could I explain how childhood wounds, innate sin, and deep-seated shame become the breeding ground of chemical, emotional, and psychological dependencies? How could I explain to a preadolescent how a deep sense of inadequacy in the unaffirmed soul creates a gnawing anxiety that craves to be masked? I decided to keep it simple.

"Bennett, as strange as it may sound, that pro golfer isn't happy, and he's looking for a way to feel better. Even though he's rich and famous and gets to play golf all the time, deep down he doesn't feel good about himself."

It was quiet for a long moment.

"Well," Bennett said with confidence and a slow, happy drawl, "I lo-o-ove *my*self."

After I muffled my laughter and silently thanked God, I simply responded, "Good, Bennett. As long as you love yourself you'll probably never be addicted to anything."

I was still smiling as we made our way down the first fairway, thanking God that my boy loved himself.

There was a time in my life when I thought that loving yourself was the same thing as being self-centered. Because self-centeredness is ungodly, it wasn't a great leap to unconsciously conclude that loving myself was sinful.

When I learned about the power of blessing, I began to realize how often I had cursed myself under the guise of being humble and godly. Simply put, we only bless what we love. What we hate, we curse.

God has made you a little lower than the angels, and Christ paid the ultimate price to bless your life. You'll bring God no honor by cursing what He has blessed. If you're going to live a fruitful, joyful life, learn to bless, not curse, your own life.

You can love yourself without being self-absorbed. Self-blessing isn't a form of narcissism. It's an affirmation of authentic self-esteem.

Accepting Yourself

I ask most prospective grooms to read Charlie Shedd's classic little book *Letters to Philip*. It's a father's timeless advice to his son about how to treat a woman. I want engaged men to read it for many reasons, not the least of which is that, if they start the book at all, they will surely make it to chapter 2. Pastor Shedd tells Phil about a day that a young woman named Frances met him at his minister's study. Knowing how Pastor Shedd loved to hear success stories, the attractive, confident wife wanted to share with her pastor why she thought her mate, Mark, was the best husband in the world.

"From the day I started school," Frances began, "clear up to college, everyone made fun of my legs. As you can see, they look like tree stumps."

When she voluntarily stood up to display her legs, Pastor Shedd saw that, yes, they did look quite stocky. At the same time, he was amazed that she didn't seem embarrassed in the least by this unusual bodily feature.

"Sometimes when I was little I would cry myself to sleep. . . . In high school I dated some but never more than a couple of times with any one boy and you can guess why."

Frances soon shared how she had met Mark in college and how much she liked him right away. Though Mark never once commented on her legs, she often did. "You know, looking for assurance," she told the pastor.

One night, Mark took Frances's hands, looked her in the eye, and said, "Frances, I want you to quit knocking yourself. I love you the way you are. The Lord gave you good, sturdy legs. They give me a solid feeling and I like it."

In the atmosphere of Mark's blessing, some deep place in Frances softened, and she cried with hope and joy.

Sometime later, Mark took Frances home to meet his mother. Frances nearly melted when she saw her boyfriend's mom. She had a disability in one of her legs. She wore a built-up shoe and walked with a big limp.

"I looked at [Mark]," Frances said, "and he looked at me and I think I loved him right then like nobody ever loved a man before. . . . That was thirteen years ago and now I can honestly laugh about my legs. Can you see why I say he's wonderful? There isn't one thing in the world I wouldn't do for Mark!"[1]

Until that marvelous moment, Mark loved Frances, but Frances didn't love herself. He could bless her, but she couldn't bless herself.

It's possible to be acceptable and not know it. If we don't believe ourselves accepted, we remain afraid. What we refuse to accept, we curse.

Mark's love, as priceless and beautiful as it was, didn't cure Frances's insecurity. It was only when Frances accepted herself that her fear was banished.

Imagine an unemployed man interviewing for a job. He's been unemployed for so long and rejected by so many potential employers that he has a hard time believing anything good is going to happen. "I'll probably get rejected again," he tells himself.

With no blessing of self, the unemployed man enters the interview with low confidence. But what does the potential employer want most in this prospective employee? Confidence. The employer is looking for someone who is comfortable in his own skin, confident of his abilities, and brimming with a positive, hopeful outlook. The interviewee may be the most skilled man for the job, but, obscured by the cloak of insecurity, he's unlikely to be offered it.

Where there is no blessing of self, our souls are battered into insecurity, our confidence dies, and we become prone to fail at what we otherwise could easily accomplish. The inability to accept and love ourselves may be the single greatest obstacle to living the blessed life God intends for us.

What? Lack of self-love is the big problem in our generation? Isn't this a generation of people in love with themselves? Isn't today's problem not a lack of self-love but an epidemic of it?

Let's take a look at one of Jesus's most famous stories for the answer.

Two Heirs, Two Errors, One Root Problem

It has been labeled the parable of the prodigal son, but it is the father who is prodigal (lavishly excessive), and the story is as much about the older brother as it is about the younger. Woven into Jesus's famous, simple parable is an exquisite portrait of the power of self-curse and the road to self-blessing.

> There was a man who had two sons. And the younger of them said to his father, "Father, give me the share of property that is coming to me." And he divided his property between them. (Luke 15:11–12)

The younger son's request conveyed his heart—he would rather his father have been dead. He had no interest in a relationship with his dad. He was interested only in what he could grab for himself.

> Not many days later, the younger son gathered all he had and took a journey into a far country, and there he squandered his property in reckless living. And when he had spent everything, a severe famine arose in that country, and he began to be in need. So he went and hired himself out to one of the citizens of that country, who sent him into his fields to feed pigs. And he was longing to be fed with the pods that the pigs ate, and no one gave him anything. (Luke 15:13–16)

"See there," you may be quick to assert. "There is a picture of a man in love with himself. That younger brother cared only about himself. That's the problem with the world today too. Young people love themselves but nobody else."

He loved himself? Really?

Think of the person you love most in the world. Who do you envision? A son or daughter? A husband or wife? A best friend? Would you ever, in your wildest imagination, on your worst day, do to the one you love what the younger brother did to himself? Would you ever lead someone you love into abject rebellion? Would you ever counsel someone you love to reject the blessings of home, heritage, and family? Would you ever curse someone you love with the folly of wasteful living? Would you ever relegate someone you love to the prostitutes and pigpens?

Of course not. You would only do those things to someone you hated. You curse what you hate. You bless what you consider valuable.

This might be one of the most sobering questions you've ever considered: would you ever treat someone you love the way you sometimes treat yourself?

The younger brother's waywardness, like all folly, flowed from self-loathing, not self-love. Only those who place little value on their lives live self-destructively.

The younger son's problem was not self-love. It was self-absorption.

Like the mythical figure Narcissus, who fell in love with his image reflected in the water, self-consumed souls are obsessed with their image precisely because they are discontent with themselves. Obsessing about ourselves is not blessing ourselves. When we accept ourselves, we don't need to think about ourselves all the time. As C. S. Lewis pointed out in his classic *Mere Christianity*, if you meet a truly humble person, "he will not be thinking about humility: he will not be thinking about himself at all."[2]

When we are constantly considering our image, worrying and wondering what others think of us, we can be sure that the ego, the deepest inner self, is hurting. Tim Keller puts it this way: "Have you ever thought about the fact that you do not notice your body until there is something wrong with it?

When we are walking around, we are not usually thinking how fantastic our toes are feeling. . . . That is because the parts of our body only draw attention to themselves if there is something wrong with them."[3] If we're constantly focused on ourselves and puff ourselves up in the eyes of others, we aren't practicing self-blessing. We're revealing a wounded ego. The rampant self-absorption we see in society is not the fruit of self-love. It's the consequence of self-hatred.

The Cycle of Self-Hatred and Curse

Most of us instinctively know that the world is founded on justice. In order for things to be fair, good must be rewarded and bad must be punished. Seeing the bad within ourselves, we make sure things turn out fair by punishing ourselves. When we see our flaws, our ugliness, and our failures, we want to do something to correct them. But when we have no success in conquering our sin, we appoint ourselves our own judge, examine the evidence, and issue the verdict: condemned. Once we condemn ourselves, it only stands to reason that we announce a negative future for the one condemned.

Once, after a moment of juvenile frustration and failure, one of my kids asked me, "Dad, is it a sin to say I stink at this?"

My response was simple: "Would it be a sin for you to tell one of your friends, 'You stink at this'?"

Sometimes we need to turn the Golden Rule around. Do unto yourself what you would do unto others. Christians have no problem admitting that it's wrong to criticize and put down others, but we so readily curse ourselves. Why?

The human mind longs for order. We want to make sense out of the world. We want things to line up the way they should. When we curse ourselves, we are simply giving voice to a logical conclusion: *I've seen my sin and my failures, and clearly, anyone with that many flaws can't succeed in life.*

When too much blessing comes, we get nervous and superstitious. We might say things like, "No one in the family has been sick in over a year—knock on wood." And isn't it strange how unsettled we feel in our times of prosperity? "Well, I'm sure the other shoe will drop soon." Most of us are uncomfortable even saying something positive about ourselves. It feels somehow wrong to say, "I'm going to do well at this job" or "I am good at my work."

On the other hand, we find it easy to rehearse our negative forecasts mentally. We're bent toward envisioning future failures. When we curse ourselves consistently enough, ironically, we unconsciously want to prove our forecasts true. Once we've judged ourselves, condemned ourselves, and cursed ourselves, we unconsciously punish ourselves to prove the curse.

The longer I live, the more I suspect that self-sabotage is my worst enemy.

Self-Sabotage

I played tennis as a kid. I loved the game and played it almost every day of my growing-up years. I was ranked in the top fifteen players in my state as a junior tennis player and was honored as the tennis MVP of our large high school my senior year. But as much as I loved the game and as hard as

I practiced, there was always something holding me back from reaching the top ten in the state.

When you get to a certain level in any junior sport, you get to know your competitors. I knew who had a good serve, who had a weak backhand, and who made dishonest calls. But the main thing I knew was whether they were ranked ahead of me, which usually meant they were seeded ahead of me in the tournament.

It was ridiculous, but I figured that the rankings gave me enough information to determine whom I was going to beat and who was going to beat me. I always knew where I stood. If I was ranked higher than my opponent, I felt a bit nervous because I was supposed to win. But I would usually overcome my nerves and win. If I was ranked lower than my opponent, I would play hard, but deep inside I had already rehearsed the probable failure and almost always lost. This dreadful thought process greatly limited my ability to ascend in the rankings. I just couldn't envision myself beating the top ten guys—so I never did. It sounds silly and simplistic, but if we tell ourselves that we'll probably fail, we'll usually find a way to fail in order prove to ourselves that we aren't liars.

That was my tennis mindset until I started focusing on playing doubles with Andy. I was a short, quick kid and Andy was a tall, lanky kid. We were a strange sight but a good blend of talent. Andy had a powerful serve and over-head smash, while I had a quick step to cover the court and a consistent topspin forehand. I needed Andy's height and power, but far and away, the thing I needed most from him was his crazy mind. He was a super-intelligent kid with academic prowess, but sometimes I thought he was just too dumb to recognize who was better than us.

"Andy, do you know who we play this week? These guys are ranked second in the state."

"So what? Big deal. We can beat them. They're no better than us."

"But, Andy, they're ranked second. You really think we can beat them?"

"Of course we can."

We won a lot of matches not because *I* believed we could win but because I believed that *Andy* believed we could. Eventually, for the first time in my tennis career, I quit assuming I'd lose to higher-ranked players. I became almost as dumb as Andy and started thinking that we could beat almost anybody! By the year's end, we'd won the North Carolina Eastern regional, and we were the number-one seed in the state high school tournament.

If I could sabotage myself in something as trivial as tennis, what about all the important arenas of life? How many other ways have I unconsciously defeated myself?

We should pay attention to our recurring errors because self-sabotage may be at work.

A woman finds herself in one abusive relationship after another. Why is she choosing men who hurt her? She's keeping her rank.

A man loses job after job making the same sorts of errors. Why does he stumble every time when the job seems to be going well? He's keeping his rank.

A couple finally gets their finances in order and then makes another bad investment. Why do they continually make bad financial decisions? They're keeping their rank.

I needed an Andy to plant the liberating thought, *Maybe I can play at a higher level.* Frances needed Mark's acceptance to set her free from the ranking system. Ultimately, we all need to find ourselves accepted "in the Beloved" (Eph. 1:6) if we're ever going to escape the cycle of self-sabotage.

Blessing Your Own Life

The prodigal's return home was a move toward blessing. There was no blessing for him in the pigpen. As he was considering eating the hog slop, he remembered the smell of lamb chops on his father's grill. When "he came to his senses" (Luke 15:17 NIV), his self-absorption began to melt as he simply thought of someone outside himself.

The beginning of blessing yourself is the contemplation of your heavenly Father's affection. Those who move toward God's grace bless themselves.

"Here I am starving to death! I will set out and go back," the younger son said (vv. 17–18 NIV). In his contrition and repentance, he was revealing the beginning steps of self-acceptance: *I have failed. I have scandalized the family. I am unworthy. But my life is not over. I can go back. I can start over. I have failed utterly, but I do not have to condemn myself to a pigpen prison for the rest of my life. I will be honest with my father about my failures and my unworthiness, and perhaps he will accept me anyway.*

Self-blessing depends upon accepting oneself, and self-acceptance is born from Another's acceptance. We can only accept ourselves when someone greater demonstrates to us that we are acceptable. We can only bless ourselves when we believe in the blessing of one greater than ourselves.

The younger son's risky move toward his father was not a manipulative, religious stunt. The son was, probably for the first time in his life, able to really be himself. There was greater joy in the simple freedom of being real with his dad than in all the parties, promiscuity, and popularity combined. Oh, the sweet freedom of finally being yourself: *Here I am, Father. Broken, humiliated, hungry, and needing to be held.*

I recently saw an image that sums up the transformation in the younger son's life:

Religion says, "I messed up. My father is going to be so mad." The Gospel says, "I messed up; better call Dad."

It wasn't the robe, the ring, the sandals, and the fattened calf that changed the son. It was the father's heart. It was a daddy accepting his boy. The boy had left home wanting to assert his independence, wanting to prove that he was "all grown up." But it was there, weeping in his father's arms, that the boy became a man.

In the end, it wasn't a complicated, mystical self-realization that the son needed. He needed identification with his father. Contrary to the popular self-esteem movements of recent decades, the path to self-acceptance, ironically, is not found within ourselves. If we look within ourselves in order to accept ourselves, we'll despair when we see our sins, our failures, and our ugliness. The wayward son didn't one day look within himself and find an inward holiness that boosted his esteem. Instead, the boy went to his father. It was in his father's arms that he found his worth.

He had rehearsed his soliloquy of repentance, but his lavish father interrupted the speech and began the celebration.

As scandalous as it seems, there was no penance demanded, no religious gestures required, and no repayment requested.

For the first time since the foolish son had started his riotous living, he was no longer absorbed with himself. Suddenly, his life wasn't about his own image. *What do people think of me? Am I popular? Do I look successful? Am I happy?* Instead, his life was rooted in his father's affection. *I belong to him. I belong here. My father loves me. I matter. I am accepted.*

Accept Christ's blessing and you can bless yourself. Accept the fact that Christ was alienated for you and you can quit rejecting yourself. Accept the fact that Christ was cursed for you and you can quit cursing yourself. Accept the fact that Jesus was crucified for you and you can quit crucifying yourself.

If her husband's acceptance empowered Frances to finally love herself, how much more powerful is the heavenly groom's acceptance of you? Christ, knowing every defect of yours, came in love to die for you. Because you are forever accepted in the Beloved, you can finally, fully accept rather than reject yourself. When you most feel like cursing yourself is when you most need to agree with God's assessment rather than your own feelings.

Feel like calling yourself ugly? Try *a radiant bride* (Rev. 21:2).

Feel like calling yourself worthless? Try a *treasure in an earthen vessel* (2 Cor. 4:7).

Feel like calling yourself unwelcome? Try *lost and now found* (Luke 15:32).

Feel like calling yourself left out? Try *a chosen one, in Christ before the foundation of the world* (Eph. 1:4).

Feel like calling yourself unshapely? Try *fearfully and wonderfully made* (Ps. 139:14).

Feel like calling yourself small? Try *the seed of a great fruit tree* (1 Pet. 1:23).

Feel like calling yourself bland? Try *the salt of the earth* (Matt. 5:13).

Feel like calling yourself ignorant? Try declaring yourself to have *the mind of Christ* (1 Cor. 2:16).

Feel like calling yourself bound? Try *by the truth, you are free* (John 8:32).

Feel like calling yourself disconnected? Try *a branch on the True Vine* (John 15:1).

Feel like calling yourself dirty? Try *whiter than snow* (Ps. 51:7).

Feel like calling yourself mundane? Try *God's holy temple* (Eph. 2:21).

Feel like calling yourself unemployable? Try *God's co-laborer* (2 Cor. 6:1).

Feel like calling yourself poor? Try *spiritually rich in every way* (Eph. 1:7).

Feel like calling yourself unneeded? Try *a member of Christ's body* (1 Cor. 12:27).

Feel like calling yourself low-class? Try *a royal priest* (1 Pet. 2:9).

Feel like calling yourself an orphan? Try *son or daughter* (John 1:12).

The Father's arms are open wide. Hear Him pleading with every son or daughter trapped in self-curse: "Come, enter the celebration. The band is playing. The lamb chops are on the grill. There's laughter in the hallways. Whether you've wandered to a faraway land or you've wearied yourself slaving in the local fields, you can come home."

Christ died to make you acceptable. In His name, accept yourself. Christ took the curse to make you blessed. In His name, you can bless your life.

10

Learning to Speak Like God

Imagine your teenage son has just wrecked your car because he was texting while driving. Thankfully, the crash didn't injure your son, but it did damage the car significantly. What's your likely knee-jerk response? I'm not asking about the manner of discipline you might apply. I'm asking what you likely would *say* to your child. Be honest with yourself. Imagine the frustrations and fears you're feeling over your son's folly. What's your gut response? Which of the following statements would you most likely say? (Not which one do you *wish* you would say, but which one would you *likely* say?)

"You're so irresponsible. I'm afraid you're going to get yourself killed."

"If you'd been paying better attention, this wouldn't have happened."

"Boys will be boys. Don't worry. It's no big deal—I'm just glad you're not hurt."

After being honest about which of the above statements would be your likely response to your child, consider another important question: Which of the statements most closely conveys the power of blessing?

It's a trick question—none of them are blessing statements.

The first declaration is a fear-based, dark forecast—a negative label and a prognostication of doom. It's what I'd call *curse*. The second statement is true, but it isn't helpful. It emphasizes the law—what *should* be done—but offers no power to do it. It's what I'd call *moralism*. And the third statement, which is so full of grace, leaves out the truth. It isn't a blessing to tell a teenager that his folly is "no big deal." It *is* a big deal when a teenager texts and drives. A response of love and acceptance that doesn't truthfully point to a better way isn't blessing. It's what I'd call *amoralism*—an absence of right and wrong.

Curse declares, "You've messed up and you're doomed."

Moralism declares, "You need to be better in order to be accepted."

Amoralism declares, "You don't need to be better—just be yourself."

But blessing is a declaration of grace and truth: "I'm so glad you aren't hurt. I love you, not the car. But you can be a better driver than this. You're smart enough to know the dangers of texting and driving. God has a great destiny planned for you, and it doesn't include distracted driving. Every time you get in the car, remember that you're my treasure, so put down the phone and drive safely."

Grace and Truth

Blessing is an act of grace—an unearned gift. It is also a declaration of truth—an announcement of authentic possibilities. As we learned in chapter 2, blessing always comes first. That's grace. Blessing is an act of grace because it isn't a reward. It's a gift. In chapter 3, we learned that blessing unveils authentic identity. Blessing points people to the highest reality about their destiny. Blessing isn't just grace and it isn't just truth. It's always both. Any form of speech that isn't both grace and truth isn't blessing.

The prologue to John's Gospel reveals something unique about Jesus: "And the Word became flesh and dwelt among us, and we have seen his glory, glory as of the only Son from the Father, full of grace and truth" (1:14). The glory of God is unveiled in the wedding of grace and truth. Jesus was full of grace and truth. He wasn't 50 percent grace and 50 percent truth. Jesus was (and is) always 100 percent grace and 100 percent truth.

Jesus was perfectly gracious and perfectly truthful, but mere mortals usually swing like a pendulum between the two virtues. Any parent can identify. When raising our kids, sometimes I felt full of grace. I was surprisingly gracious when on vacation. "You want ice cream for the sixth time in three days? Well, okay, why not? What flavor?"

But other times, when under stress or when no one had cleaned their room in weeks, my truth might easily overwhelm my grace. "No, you can't have any ice cream. We've had way too much sugar. Life takes discipline, and speaking of discipline, have you made your bed today?"

Neither unbridled permissiveness (grace without truth) nor strict rule enforcement (truth without grace) makes for effective parenting. Great parenting, of course, requires both grace and truth.

Similarly, blessing is an act of both grace and truth. It is an expression of love spoken in accord with God's Word. Blessing is an expression of imagination joined with authentic discernment.

Without truth, an affirmation isn't a blessing at all. Tim Keller describes blessing as "accurate spiritual discernment of who a person really is."[1] If an affirmation is inaccurate, it's counterproductive.

I loved peewee football, but when I graduated to the midget league (sixth grade), the big kids started crushing me. As much as I craved my dad's blessing, I'm glad he didn't bless me with a vision of becoming an NFL football player. I would have wasted a lot of time—and probably been permanently maimed.

A 2015 University of Amsterdam study on overpraising children has drawn a lot of interest because it spawned headlines such as "Too Much Praise Promotes Narcissism." Researchers followed 565 children ages seven to twelve over an eighteen-month period to explore possible correlations between parental praise and narcissistic tendencies in the children. Despite the headlines that followed the study's publication, a closer look at the research reveals that it's not overpraising a child that leads to self-absorption—it's *inaccurately* praising a child.[2]

If my father had told me I was a better football player than anyone else, it would have been wrong on at least two levels. First, I wasn't big enough to be a great football player, and second, it would've puffed up my pride rather than affirming my worth.

A parent probably can't praise a child too much, but a parent certainly can praise in an unhealthy manner. To invite a child into prideful comparisons by saying, "You are smarter than all the other students" isn't a blessing. It's an invitation to selfish, narcissistic thoughts.

Praising others without truth doesn't carry the force of blessing. It fosters a distorted view of self.

On the other hand, without grace, truth statements can be harsh and crushing. To say to a child, "If you don't study harder, you're going to fail out of school" might be true, but it isn't helpful.

I once played catcher on a church softball team despite the fact that I have no softball skills. There's no candy-coating it—I was a terrible catcher. But when the overly competitive coach yelled at me after I fumbled a tag at home base, it only made me more nervous and thus worse at catching the ball.

A friend once blessed me by describing our church as "full of grace and truth," and he doodled a diagram that I've never forgotten.[3]

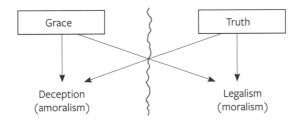

He started with the words "Grace" and "Truth" at the top of the napkin and reminded me that Jesus was *all* grace and *all* truth *all* the time. He then drew a slanted arrow from under "Grace" to below "Truth" and asked, "What is the opposite of grace?" When I suggested legalism, he wrote that below "Truth." Likewise, he asked for the word that is the opposite of truth and wrote "Deception" beneath "Grace."

He then reminded me that most Christians (and churches) tend to separate truth and grace and lean toward one side or the other. To signify the divide, he drew a squiggly line downward between the two headings. As he drew a new arrow from "Grace" to "Deception," my friend explained, "So, if you have all grace and no truth, it can lead to deception." Likewise, he drew a line from "Truth" to "Legalism" and said, "If you have all truth and no grace, you can wind up in legalism."

To be clear, grace is always good. Truth is always good. But for real transformation, we need both.

Moving toward More Grace, More Truth

It's helpful to think of grace and truth as continuums. The diagram below depicts four quadrants that are determined by the direction of grace and truth. The more full of grace and truth a blessing is, the more powerful it is. Conversely, the extreme absence of grace and truth makes a curse especially wicked. Where there is an abundance of grace but no truth, people won't feel judged, but they'll never rise beyond their feelings. Where there is an abundance of truth but no grace, people will be called to a higher standard, but they'll feel judged and coerced.

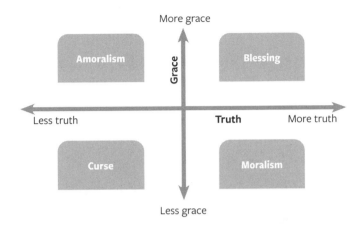

Moralism withholds blessing until you change. Amoralism asserts you don't need to change. Curse empowers you to change for the worse. Blessing empowers you to change for the better.

Here's another way to compare the quadrants: Moralism offers a positive future if you can prove you deserve it. Amoralism affirms a positive future *because* you deserve it. Curse negates a positive future because you don't deserve it. Blessing affirms a positive future that you don't deserve.

Because Jesus was perfectly full of grace and perfectly full of truth at all times, His blessing was perfectly powerful to change people for the good. Jesus came to displace the curse of hell, and He rejected not only the amoralism of the licentious Roman culture but also the moralism of the Jewish Pharisees.

The first, most important step in training yourself to bless is evaluating your speech (and evaluating every word spoken to you) by asking, *Is this blessing, moralism, amoralism, or curse?* In other words, when you're not blessing, in which quadrant do you find yourself?

As I said earlier, grace is good and truth is good. But grace without truth conveys acceptance without helping anyone change, because we need truth in order to go in the right direction. On the other hand, truth without grace points people in the right direction but, apart from grace, repels people the way the Pharisees pushed away the sinners of their day. As depicted in the diagram below, blessing and curse are both powerful and transformational, but in opposite directions.

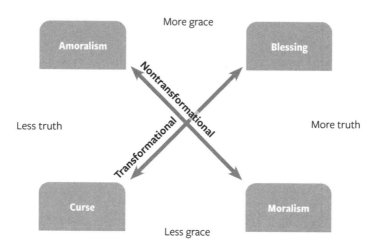

Moralism

Steinbeck's classic *East of Eden* retells the Cain and Abel story—a tale of bitter sibling rivalry and the unquenchable quest for a father's blessing. Adam Trask's son Cal is fiercely jealous of his more likable brother, Aron, who clearly has more of their father's affection. Knowing that their father lost his wealth in a harebrained refrigeration business scheme,

Cal thinks he knows the way to their father's heart—he'll make a lot of money and give it to him. Cal approaches Will Hamilton, a businessman with the Midas touch, for advice on getting rich.

"Listen—you have a brother. Does your father like him better than you?" Will asks.

"Everybody does," Cal responds.

Will later asks bluntly, "Suppose you should get this money and give it to your father—would it cross your mind that you were trying to buy his love?"

"Yes, sir. It would. And it would be true."[4]

Most moralists aren't so honest. I wasn't so honest with myself until I had graduated college and seminary and was striving to be the perfect pastor. I finally admitted to myself that my perfectionism was an unconscious attempt to make my dad proud. You can spend your whole life unconsciously trying to earn someone's blessing.

Moralism might also be called *legalism* or *religion*. If you went to Sunday school as a kid, you probably heard a lot of Bible moralism: "Be brave like David when he fought Goliath and you'll be rewarded. Don't be like Jonah—you see what happened when he ran away from God. You don't want to get swallowed by a whale, do you?" Moralism emphasizes righteousness and obedience to the neglect of love and mercy. Moralistic people, like the Pharisees, care more about being right than they do about being in relationship.

Jesus's famous parable of the prodigal son is really a story about a father who had two sons. While the riotous, younger son lacked any semblance of morality (grace without truth), the older brother was a dedicated moralist who dutifully stayed at home doing what was expected of good sons.

When the father showed lavish grace to the reunited, wayward younger son, the older brother "was angry and refused to go in" to the party (Luke 15:28). His language revealed his moralistic heart: "Look, these many years I have served you, and I never disobeyed your command, yet you never gave me a young goat" (v. 29).

The older brother never entered the celebration because moral conformity, while applauded by society, can't earn blessing. If blessing is given for obedience, it isn't blessing—it's compensation. To exhort others to moral conformity without imparting the blessing to empower them is, in Jesus's words, to "tie up heavy burdens, hard to bear, and lay them on people's shoulders" (Matt. 23:4).

The Pharisees used the truth of the law to puff themselves and put down others. Moralism puts you in charge of your own salvation. That's why Jesus hates it.

Amoralism

The younger brother, the prodigal son, took the opposite path of the older brother. He scandalized his family in order to follow his own selfish pleasures. He cared nothing for society's expectations. He assumed the path to blessedness was doing what felt good, not doing what was right.

Tim Keller has summed up the parable's portrait clearly: "Jesus uses the younger and elder brothers to portray the two basic ways people try to find happiness and fulfillment: the way of moral conformity and the way of self-discovery."[5] While the older brother typifies so much of the dead religion that a new generation in America has rejected, the younger brother typifies the spirit of the modern age. I've labeled it *amoralism* to signify how this sort of self-actualization ideology stands in direct contrast to moralism and because *amoralism* doesn't mean "anti-morality"—it means "no morality." That's the mantra of our times: "Right and wrong are relative. If it doesn't hurt anyone, then do whatever seems right to you." Amoralism is grace without truth. From the amoralist's perspective, blessing should offer affirmation but no life direction.

American culture is profoundly divided along these two lines of moralism and amoralism. Again, Tim Keller sheds light on the phenomenon:

> The moral conformists say: "The immoral people—the people who 'do their own thing'—are the problem with the world, and the moral people are the solution." The advocates of self-discovery say: "The bigoted people—the people who say, 'We have the Truth'—are the problem with the world, and progressive people are the solution."[6]

Some people, like Jacob, can swing between both wrong-minded attempts to be blessed. At times he was amoral, seeking blessing by any means, whether right or wrong. He manipulated his brother, lied to his father, and tricked his father-in-law as if he had no moral compass. At other times, he was the consummate moralist. In his glorious dream he saw a ladder connecting earth to heaven, covered with ascending and descending angels. Jacob's life was more connected to heaven than he had known! In awe and fear, he rose early the next morning and set up a stone as a religious altar. "Then Jacob made a vow, saying, 'If God will be with me and will keep me in this way that I go, and will give me bread to eat and clothing to wear . . . then the LORD shall be my God, and . . . I will give a full tenth to you'" (Gen. 28:20–22). Moralists love to make vows to God: "If you'll bless me, I'll be a good person."

Curse

A boy saw a minister repeatedly pulling on a lawn mower rope in an attempt to start the stubborn old machine and said, "Pastor, it'll start quicker if you cuss."

"Why, I'm a minister. I'm not sure I even remember how to say cuss words," the pastor responded.

"You just keep pulling on that string, Reverend, and it'll come back to you," the boy said.

The biblical notion of cursing certainly isn't what moderns mean by *cussing*. The Scriptures depict curse as the opposite of blessing: it's a dark, mystical force that can have binding power. When Jacob plotted with his mother to trick old Isaac by clothing himself with animal skins in order to mimic the hairy-armed Esau, he feared invoking a curse upon himself: "Perhaps my father will feel me, and I shall seem to be mocking him and bring a curse upon myself and not a blessing" (Gen. 27:12). Interestingly, Jacob's mother, Rebekah, revealed another deep, biblical notion—a curse can be borne by another: "His mother said to him, 'Let your curse be on me, my son'" (v. 13).

To curse is to will and speak seeds of doom toward others. If blessing is full of grace and truth, curse has neither. If blessing is a faith-filled, positive vision spoken in accord with God's Word that releases people into their destiny of productivity and dominion on the earth, curse is an ungodly, negative forecast that, when believed and received, leads toward the negative vision proclaimed.

Curse is often forged in the fires of hate, resentment, and fear. After Jacob stole Esau's blessing, Esau's instinct was to curse his brother with his name: "Is he not rightly named Jacob?" (Gen. 27:36). Since Jacob means "supplanter" or "deceiver," Esau turned it into a permanent vilification of Jacob's character. "He's just a cheater—he always has been and always will be." Hurt people hurt people, and they often use curse as the weapon.

Oddly, fear can lead people to curse even those they love. A fearful parent might try to leverage curse as the ultimate form of motivation. I know of a father who, in an attempt to instill a work ethic in his nine-year-old, told the child, "If you don't study hard and get a good job and be a good person, I'll come back from the grave someday and haunt you."

It's a sinful delusion to think we can motivate someone toward good by declaring them bad. Why would a wife think she could spur her husband into greater emotional intimacy by saying, "You can't ever share your feelings"? Why would a husband think he's going to motivate his wife toward a more fulfilling sex life by calling her unattractive? James described the problem of the tongue: "With it we bless our Lord and Father, and with it we curse people who are made in the likeness of God. From the same mouth come blessing and cursing. My brothers, these things ought not to be so" (James 3:9–10).

If we want to get rid of all forms of cursing, we need to pay attention to statements that begin with, "I/you can't . . . ," "I'm/ you're too . . . ," "I'll/you'll never . . . ," and "I/you always . . .":

I can't get over this cold.
I can't control my temper.
I can't win for losing.

I'm too old for that.
I'm too dumb to figure it out.
I'm too poor to ever get ahead.

I'll never get over it.
I'll never get another chance like that.
I'll never be able to face him/her.

You're always late.
You're always in trouble.
You always talk too much.

Isn't it also odd that, as much as we all want to live long and healthy lives, we incorporate death into so many of our figures of speech? It's best to get rid of death speech, even the terms we mean in jest or for emphasis:

I'm dying to see you.
I'm as serious as a heart attack.
I'm dead serious.
I'm just tickled to death.
You're killing me.
Cross my heart and hope to die.
Just go out there and knock 'em dead.

Family mottoes, those sayings that we heard our parents repeat over and over, also can carry a subtle message of curse:

If it's not one thing, it's another.
I'm just waiting for the other shoe to drop.
You made your bed, now you have to lie in it.
The road to hell is paved with good intentions.

The more a curse is believed, the more binding power it has. If a toddler spills her milk and her mother says, "You're so clumsy. You're always spilling things and messing up Mommy's nice clean floor," the child doesn't know how to categorize the statement. Two-year-olds don't say to themselves, *Well, Mom just spoke a little curse there because she is having a stressful day. I'm only two, and I don't have the manual dexterity she would like me to have. It's not really my problem. I'm sure Mom will work it out with her therapist later.* Toddlers don't think that way, do they? No, they just believe what authorities say about them.

We've all had forms of curse spoken into our lives. It's important to recognize the curses and reject them in full confidence that, in Christ, we aren't cursed—we're blessed. Christ came not only to forgive our sins by taking the punishment due us but also to bless our lives by taking the curse due us. Paul made it clear: "Christ redeemed us from the curse of the law by becoming a curse for us—for it is written, 'Cursed is everyone who is hanged on a tree'—so that in Christ Jesus the blessing of Abraham might come to the Gentiles, so that we might receive the promised Spirit through faith" (Gal. 3:13–14).

The more deeply we receive the gospel and know ourselves blessed, the less any curse will have power over us. "Like a fluttering sparrow or a darting swallow, an undeserved curse does not come to rest" (Prov. 26:2 NIV). Anyone who accepts Christ's redeeming work is undeserving of the curse. Curses can't light upon us when all our wrongdoing has been utterly expunged from the record book. In an unthinkable, glorious exchange, Christ bore the curse on the cross so that we will bear His blessing forever. We can live so confidently in our blessedness that curse can't roost in our souls.

Early in our marriage, Anne was awakened one night by an obscene phone caller, but sweet Anne had never heard such a call and assumed the best. The caller spoke in a raspy whisper.

"What?" Anne asked.

The caller continued with his muffled whispers.

Anne asked, "What did you say?"

He whispered a little louder.

Still, Anne naively asked, *"What?"*

"Lady, can you not hear me?" the caller finally said in a plain voice.

"Oh, I can hear you now," my wife responded.

"Never mind," the caller said in frustration as he hung up.

Anne was so naive and innocent regarding the obscenity that the ugly language didn't even register with her. The caller wanted to draw her into his darkness, but his obscene speech was, as the proverb described, "like a fluttering sparrow"—it could not "come to rest."

When we are unconvinced that we are thoroughly forgiven, curse tries to connect to the seeds of condemnation we already feel. But when we revel in our righteousness in Christ, we become immune to curse.

If haters or fearful people have cursed your life, you can recognize it, renounce it, and replace every curse with blessing.

The Blessing I Needed

Because I began the book by sharing how much I craved my father's affirmation, you might think that the blessing I most needed from him was acceptance. But looking back, I realize that the blessing I most wanted was not his endorsement but his correction. I craved his direction.

One of the most formative (and cherished) interactions I recall with my father was a form of correction done well. I was perhaps nine years old, and we were walking to the car after he'd coached my peewee football game. The football fields were adjacent to a city park, and as we approached the parking lot, we saw a middle-aged African American man sitting at a picnic table reading a book. As did most people in my home city, the man recognized my TV newsman father and spoke to him. Dad was humble and never acted like a celebrity—I liked that about him.

My father politely stopped to talk. The man at the picnic table explained that he'd gone back to school. He was learning to read.

"I want to be better than Martin Luther King," the barely literate man said.

As we walked to the car, I unthinkingly mocked the man. "Humph," I said. "He can barely read and he wants to be better than Martin Luther King."

Instead of joining in my mockery, my father said solemnly, "I think that's a very noble goal for him to have, Son." We walked silently the rest of the way to the car.

Other than the memories of my dad giving me the rapid-towel treatment he called "the drying machine" after my bath when I was a preschooler or the spy stories he wove at bedtime, that day at the city park, when my father blessed a black man and corrected me, is probably my favorite memory of him. To my knowledge, I never again mocked in thought, word, or deed a disenfranchised person.

Some have had a lot of truth instilled in them to the neglect of grace. Some have been given grace but little truth. And some have been given little of either.

But no one has to stay stuck in moralism, amoralism, or curse. You can train your tongue to bless anyone.

11

You Can Learn to Bless Anyone

In *Everybody, Always*, Bob Goff simplifies our job: "Don't tell people what they want: tell them who they are."[1] That's what blessing does—it gives you a way to tell anybody, anywhere, anytime who they really are. You don't need a formal occasion to bless someone, and your blessing statements don't need to be flowery in order to be powerful.

I remember a round of golf I played with Bennett when he was about twelve. He started the round with a bad hole—a double bogey. His face turned red with frustration. Every golfer knows the feeling—a compelling emotion tries to convince you that chucking your clubs into the lake will make you happier. But somehow, young Bennett fought off the frustration, threw no clubs, and with surprising composure played a good round despite the ugly start.

During our conversation on the way home, I casually said, "Bennett, today when you made that double bogey to start your round, I could see you were frustrated. I know how it feels. You could have let your frustration take over, but instead, you kept your mind in the game and went on to play a good round of golf. The Bible has a word for that kind of virtue—'self-control.' In my experience, people who have a lot of self-control go far in this world. Bennett, I see you growing into a young man who is full of self-control, and I think it's going to help you succeed in life."

A lot of people feel like they're too busy to bless others or that they just aren't eloquent enough. I just reread that statement to Bennett out loud and timed it—it's twenty-eight seconds. You're never too busy to bless someone.

I also hope you noticed how simple my blessing of Bennett's self-control was—there wasn't a fancy word in it. Blessings don't need to be long or poetic, and they don't need to be shared in a formal setting. A half-minute blessing using simple words on the way home from a golf course has the power to bless. Indeed, Bennett grew up to be a man of excellent self-control. Even in undergraduate school, he developed a chart planning how many hours he would study for each course each day and stuck to it. That sort of self-control can take a student far.

Of course, when I saw Bennett's face get red with frustration on the golf course, I could have responded with moralism, amoralism, or even curse. The moralistic response always appeals to the rules. It emphasizes conditional approval and often uses "if/then" language. Here's an example of a moralistic response: "Bennett, if you want me to support your golf, you better not lose your temper on the course. If you lose control, not only will you play poorly, but I'll take your clubs from you." As we learned in the last chapter, moralistic responses emphasize the truth (it *is* true that an ill-tempered golfer plays poorly), but there is no grace. Legalistic responses always emphasize conformity to the rules as a condition for full acceptance.

Or I could have responded to Bennett's frustration with the posture of amoralism. As we learned in the last chapter, amoralism says there is no right or wrong. An amoralistic response to the frustrated golfer would emphasize acceptance while downplaying the truth: "Bennett, golf is a frustrating game. I've thrown my clubs plenty of times. I understand if you lose your cool—just make sure you never hurt yourself or someone else." If I responded like that, Bennett would have felt accepted, but he would have experienced no power for transformation.

Though in this instance Bennett showed great composure, he wasn't always so cool and collected. From time to time, when I saw him get frustrated on the golf course, it was tempting to speak curse: "Bennett, you're too frustrated. You're going to have a miserable round with that kind of attitude." Curse, as we've learned, has little truth or grace in it and leads toward destruction.

A Blessing for Every Situation

Okay, it's time to put what you've learned into practice. Below I've drawn up some hypothetical situations. I'd like you to read the scenario and then, without reading ahead, do your best to think how you would bless a person in that situation. Don't skip a scenario because it doesn't seem to apply to your life situation—there's something to be learned from every vignette. Then read on and see my descriptions of how moralism, amoralism, and curse might sound versus the power of blessing.

Scenario 1: A parent of an underachieving high school student. Your high schooler is capable of making A's and B's but has brought home a report card full of C's because he hasn't been studying diligently. How do you motivate him?

Moralism: "You better bring up your grades or else you won't get into a good college and get a good job one day. You don't see your brother coming home with C's, do you?"

Amoralism: "Don't worry about your report card. Grades aren't that important. What matters is that you follow your heart."

Curse: "You never study. You've become lazy, and it's ruining your academic transcript. No good college is going to accept you."

Blessing: "I care about you far more than your grades. You're mine and I love you no matter what. But I also know that God has given you a good mind, and I believe that you're going to make a wonderful impact in the world using that good brain of yours. We're not going to obsess over this report card—it's in the past—but I know you can develop some better study habits, so I'm going to help you make a plan."

Scenario 2: A wife of an emotionally distant husband. You have a good, responsible husband, but you wish he would share his thoughts and feelings more intimately with you. How do you help him grow?

Moralism: "You need to share your feelings more with me because that's what good husbands do. Remember, the Bible says you're supposed to love me as Christ loved the church."

Amoralism: Instead of confronting her husband, the wife thinks, *Typical man . . . doesn't like to share his emotions. I just gotta let him be.*

Curse: "You never talk to me. You're such an emotionally distant person—you just can't share your feelings, and it's ruined any chance of us having a good marriage."

Blessing: "I love hearing your thoughts because you have rich insights. And I enjoy hearing how you feel about things because you have a lot of depth. Whatever is on your heart and mind matters to me—I hope you'll share more with me."

Scenario 3: A friend of a guilt-ridden, recent divorcee. Your Christian friend has been through a painful divorce that has left her discouraged and racked with guilt over the failed marriage, which has scarred her children as well. How will you help her heal?

Moralism: "The Bible says if we confess our sins, God will forgive us. I encourage you to make sure you've repented of your part in the marital breakdown and consider this an opportunity to improve your own character."

Amoralism: "Congratulations on your newfound freedom! Enjoy your new life. Whatever you do, don't beat yourself up over it, and don't worry about the children. Kids are resilient."

Curse: "Welcome to the divorced club. It's a stigma that you have to get used to wearing. You'll probably want to watch for emotional warning signs in your children because kids from broken homes always seem to struggle."

Blessing: "There's no sin too big for God to forgive. He loves to make beauty from ashes. Though this divorce wasn't God's plan or yours, I'm convinced that He can use these painful life events for your good, for your children's good, and for His own glory."

Scenario 4: An employee with an unpleasant, negative coworker. Your coworker, in a position lateral to yours, regularly complains, is critical of you and others, and generally makes the workplace more negative. How can you correct them?

Moralism: "Do you see anyone else around here being so negative? Your critical spirit is damaging us all. If you can't snap out of this negativity, I'll have no choice but to write up a complaint with our supervisor in accord with our policy manual."

Amoralism: "You have a right to your opinions. It's never wrong to share your feelings, even if they're negative."

Curse: "You're a downer. You're always negative and never have anything positive to say. Your negative attitude has ruined the workplace for me."

Blessing: "I know our work isn't always easy or fun, but I like to make it as fulfilling as it can be, and I'd love your help. I think you can help create a more positive atmosphere. As you express your more positive side, we'll enjoy our work more and be more successful."

Scenario 5: A mother with a preschooler who has disobeyed and endangered herself. Your four-year-old likes cutting construction paper but doesn't want to use her safety scissors; she wants to use the "grown-up scissors." You've caught her with the sharp scissors. What do you say when you discipline her?

Moralism: "If you want to do fun things like cutting, you have to obey me. I don't like it when you disobey me, and God doesn't like it either."

Amoralism: "Look at you being so grown up and using Mommy's big scissors and making such good art! But Mommy needs to use her big scissors for a while, so will you try yours?"

Curse: "You never listen to me. One of these days you're going to really hurt yourself with those sharp scissors."

Blessing: "Sweetie, one day you'll be old enough to handle the big sharp scissors just fine, but they aren't safe for you to use right now. The big scissors are for big hands and the little scissors are for little hands. You are so precious to me. I don't want you to be hurt by big scissors, so I can't let you use them. But you can make beautiful things using your little scissors."

Scenario 6: A high school basketball coach addressing his underachieving team. You coach varsity basketball at a 3A high school, and your team is on a five-game losing streak because of a shooting slump. How do you get their game going in the right direction?

Moralism: "If you expect to get any playing time, you better start making more shots. And until you improve, you can expect a lot of extra sprints at every practice."

Amoralism: "Everyone goes through slumps. It's just a game, so don't take it too seriously."

Curse: "Nobody on the team can get the ball in the basket. At this rate we'll probably lose ten games in a row and be the laughingstock of the conference."

Blessing: "We may have lost five games in a row, but I still feel like I'm in a room with winners. I've seen you hit bucket after bucket in practice. I know you can make shots in the game. Forget the past five games—they're over. You're going to start making some shots, and when you do, the winning will take care of itself."

Scenario 7: A parent with a distraught teenage daughter who is pregnant. Your daughter has just confessed that she's pregnant. You didn't even know she was sexually active. She's in tears, saying that she's ruined her life. You're in shock. How do you help your daughter move forward in the midst of such unsettling news?

Moralism: "How could you have done such a thing? You know that sex outside of marriage is wrong in

God's eyes. And it's so irresponsible—didn't you think about this possibility when you went to bed with that boy?"

Amoralism: "Honey, don't cry. It's okay. Almost everyone your age is sexually active. Sometimes mistakes happen. You can choose whatever you want to do. The main thing to remember is that this doesn't make you a bad person, and it doesn't have to change any of your life plans."

Curse: "Ugh. I always worried this would happen. You're so irresponsible. How humiliating for us all. You don't have any idea how much you've messed up your life and ours."

Blessing: "Sweetheart, we love you, and there's nothing you could ever do to make us love you any less. Like you, we're in shock, and it's scary to wonder what life will be like now. But know this—your mistake is in the past, and you can move forward knowing that God is bigger than all our sins. He has good plans for you and for this baby. Today we all feel sad and anxious, but that will change. We'll be fine by the grace of God as we take it one day at a time."

Scenario 8: A husband who wishes his wife didn't nag so much. You've been married to the same woman for twenty years, and you've grown weary of her nagging about how unavailable you are. How can you help your overly critical wife become more gracious toward you?

Moralism: "You need to respect me like the Bible says. You say that I don't do enough around the house and

I don't talk to you enough. Well, maybe if you didn't nag so much I'd feel like being around you more."

Amoralism: "I know that you feel I'm not available enough, and you have a right to your opinions. I'm not perfect and I never will be. I try to accept you the way you are. I hope you'll be able to accept me as I am."

Curse: "You're a constant nag, and it's driving me nuts. No husband wants to be around a nagging wife. Your nonstop criticism has worn me out and pushed me away. I don't see any hope for our marriage."

Blessing: "I hear what you're saying, and I'd like to be more helpful and available to you. But when you speak critically to me, it doesn't help. You aren't a critical person by nature—you have encouraged me so many times over the years. You can build me up better than anyone else because you're the most important person in the world to me. God can give you grace to communicate with me in a more positive manner, and He can give me grace to become a better husband."

Crafting a Personal Blessing

All of the above examples are, of course, abbreviated, hypothetical vignettes. Deep personal blessing carries more power when you become a treasure hunter who accurately discerns someone's unique identity and potential. You can learn to mine the gold in others' souls.

To help you see and believe the best for others, I've outlined four simple steps for crafting a personal blessing and given you a model to follow. But first, remember that prayer and God's Word are the most important spiritual discernment tools you'll ever have.

Powerful blessing starts with prayer. Because it is a form of partnership with God, you can be sure that when you bless others, you are doing what God already loves to do. It's always God's will for you to bless others. "Prayer," Martin Luther said, is not "overcoming God's reluctance; it is laying hold of His willingness."[2] When it comes to blessing others' lives, God is eager for you to see people as He sees them. Ask for His help. Ask Him to grant you authentic discernment. Ask Him to empower you to love the person as He loves them.

Blessing is rooted in God's Word. Let the Scriptures be not only your guide but also your inspiration in blessing others. In appendix A, I've listed a wonderful assortment of blessings and identity statements in the Scriptures that you can incorporate into your blessing of others. You can adapt them and turn them into spoken blessings by putting them in the second person. For example, you might use John 3:16 to say, "God so loved you that He gave His only begotten Son to die for you. You're that loved." Our blessing of others is by no means limited to Scripture quotes, but it is only true and powerful if it is consistent with God's Word. When you prepare to bless others, pray for the Holy Spirit to guide you, and let the Word of God undergird everything you say.

Step 1: Remember the Essentials of the Ephraim and Manasseh Blessing

As we've learned, the mysterious Ephraim and Manasseh blessing reveals essential gifts that can serve as a road map for the ways you bless others.

Jacob adopted his grandsons as his own sons. He made them secure. He made them heirs. He assured them that they belonged. He gave them a permanent place in the family.

When you bless someone, let your first thought be, *How can my blessing help this person become more secure in God's love and mine?* If the recipient is a Christian, find ways to say, "You were chosen in Christ before the foundation of the world. You belong to God. He has adopted you and will never leave you." If the recipient has yet to receive Christ, it is always true to say, "God loves you, and because He made you, you belong to Him. He wants you!"

Manasseh means "forgotten all my troubles." To bless others to be as Manasseh is to assure them that past failures, disappointments, and painful experiences do not define them. Think about the ways your blessing can help people break free. Blessing heals people because it empathizes rather than judges. Shame researcher Brené Brown has called empathy "the strongest antidote for shame." Taking an image from a science lab, Brown asserts, "If you put shame in a petri dish and douse it with empathy, shame loses power and starts to fade."[3] Blessing people as Manasseh helps them put their lives into the perspective of Romans 8:28: "And we know that for those who love God all things work together for good, for those who are called according to his purpose."

Ephraim means "twice fruitful." When you bless others, you help them envision a fruitful future. Your blessing helps them see who they really are so that, as they discover their gifts and virtues, they are empowered to bear much fruit. Blessing moves a person's vision beyond the immediate, beyond the present circumstances. When you bless, you release people into a destiny they might not otherwise fulfill.

Jacob crossed his arms and showed favor to the undeserving one. To bless someone in the model of Ephraim and Manasseh is to affirm the unmerited favor of God. Blessing finds a thousand ways to say, "You are favored not because of your qualifications but because of God's grace." When you bless a Christian, you can confidently affirm, "You have been blessed with every spiritual blessing in Christ" (see Eph. 1:3). When you bless someone who has yet to receive Christ, you can confidently say, "God's grace is always with you. The best things in your life won't come because of your own merits but because of God's grace."

Step 2: Highlight Others' Virtues That You See More Clearly Than They Do

When I told twelve-year-old Bennett that I saw a lot of self-control in him, I simply made him aware of a quality that perhaps he would have never noticed himself. When you bless, you excavate hidden wealth, and then with joy you say, "Look at this gold I've discovered in your life."

You can become a student of others' gifts. Watch how God uses others. Listen to their dreams. Start keeping a list of the treasures you discern in them.

Here's a simple exercise: Think of someone you know and love. Consider a virtue, gift, or life opportunity that you see more clearly in that person than they see in themselves. Then use that knowledge to bless them.

I like to lead premarital couples through this simple exercise as I teach them how to bless one another. I ask the prospective bride and groom to write down one virtue they see in the other more vividly than their partner does. Sometimes the simplest blessings are the most powerful. I remember when a groom shared simply, "Honey, I believe you can make good decisions," and his fiancée burst into tears. She had always condemned herself for being indecisive, but he saw her differently and it changed her whole outlook.

Step 3: Affirm True Identity

Blessing doesn't stop at identifying unnoticed virtues and life opportunities. It globalizes the meaning of those positive qualities by assigning authentic identity. When I told Bennett that I had noticed how well he controlled himself on the golf course, I went on to generalize the virtue as part of his total personality. In other words, like Adam properly naming the animals, I accurately named Bennett: "You're a self-controlled person."

When Peter affirmed the divinity of Christ, Jesus first blessed that confession of faith, saying, "Blessed are you, Simon Bar-Jonah!" Then He gave Simon a new name: "You are Peter, and on this rock I will build my church" (Matt. 16:17–18). In other words, blessing becomes more powerful when we not only say, "I see this valuable quality in your life," but we also say, "This is the kind of special person you are."

In their classic book *The Gift of the Blessing*, Gary Smalley and John Trent suggest using "word pictures"[4] to bless others in the manner that Jacob did with his twelve sons. He called Judah "a lion's cub" (Gen. 49:9), Naphtali "a doe let loose" (v. 21), and Joseph a "fruitful bough" (v. 22). When

Jesus called Simon a rock, He was blessing him with a vivid word picture. From that time on, whenever someone called Peter's name, the disciple remembered that Jesus declared him rock-solid.

We saw earlier that when little John Wesley was saved from the devastating house fire, his mother, Susanna, used a powerful word picture when she called him "a brand plucked from the burning." One married couple blessed their baby girl born December 25 by attaching a lasting word picture: "You're the best Christmas gift!"[5]

Step 4: Attach Positive Possibilities to the Identity

When I blessed Bennett after seeing his self-control on the golf course, I didn't just affirm that virtue and generalize it as part of his identity. I went a step further: I attached the virtue to a positive future by saying, "I've noticed that self-controlled people go far in this world. I think your self-control is going to help you succeed in life."

When you point others to a positive future, you activate hope in their souls. Remember the story about Abby practicing her first speech in front of me in our living room? I highlighted her gift by saying, "Abby, I see a communication gift in you!" But I didn't stop there. I also affirmed it as part of her identity: "You are a wonderful communicator, and you have a very special way with words." Then, without overstepping, I attached future possibilities to my blessing: "Abby, God can really use a communicator like you to inspire and help people. The world is shaped by the words of great communicators."

BLESSING WORKSHEET

In preparing to bless someone, begin with prayer:

Lord, show me the ways I can bless [name]. Give me Your eyes to see them as You do. Help me show them that they're profoundly secure, free, released into a fruitful life, and walking in Your favor. Open their heart to receive the blessing. Let Isaac's words of old come true again: "I have blessed him and indeed he shall be blessed." I pray in Jesus's name, amen.

I. **Write down words or phrases that come to mind as you consider each of the essentials of the Ephraim and Manasseh blessing.**

A. Security/Belonging

(Examples: "I love spending time with you on the golf course." "You're always going to be my friend." "You could never do anything to make me stop loving you.")

_____

_____

_____

_____

_____

B. Forgiveness/Freedom
(Examples: "Way to move on after making that double bogey!" "You're not stuck!" "You seem to learn from past mistakes without wallowing in them.")

_____

_____

_____

_____

C. Fruitfulness
(Examples: "You had a great round of golf today!" "Congratulations on such a great report card—God is going to use that good brain of yours." "You are really making a positive impact with your life!")

_____

_____

_____

_____

D. Favor

(Examples: "It'll be fun to see all the doors God will open for you in the future." "I see the hand of God on you." "You are talented, but there is something greater at work in your life—the favor of God!")

_____

_____

_____

_____

II. Describe a positive quality that you see in the blessing recipient more vividly than they do.

(Example from my blessing to Bennett: "You showed a lot of self-control today.")

_____

_____

_____

_____

III. Generalize the positive quality into an identity statement.

(Example: "You're becoming a young man of great self-control.")

_____

_____

_____

_____

_____

IV. Attach positive possibilities to the blessing recipient's identity.

(Example: "People with your kind of self-control go far.")

_____

_____

_____

_____

_____

A Model Blessing

Ask if the recipient is comfortable with you taking their hand or placing your hand on their shoulder.[1] Then pray this prayer:

[Name], may God make you as Ephraim and Manasseh so that you will know that you are secure, you are freed from the past, and your life will be twice fruitful as you walk in the favor of God. I've noticed some very special things about you. You _____ [describe a positive quality from Step II]. It's part of who you are. You _____ [share a positive identity statement from Step III]. I can see God using this quality to _____ [share one or more statements from Step IV]. I bless you and look forward to seeing all that God will do in your life.

No More Flying by the Seat of Your Pants!

Remember Bob, who gave Bennett the new putter? He's flown me all over the country in his plane. He flew choppers in the Vietnam jungles and has been flying planes his whole life. He's logged over 10,000 hours—that's more than a year of his life in the air. With that much experience in a plane, you know what Bob does every time he gets in one? He goes through a basic checklist of fundamentals. *Tires inflated? Check. Instruments and radios working? Check. Altimeter, flaps, fuel mixture set? Check.*

What's Bob doing? He's sticking to the fundamentals rather than flying by his feelings. You don't have to fly by the seat of your pants when you're interacting with a difficult coworker, correcting an unruly child, or comforting a disappointed spouse.

Before you speak, ask yourself, *No moralism? Check. No amoralism? Check. No curse? Check.* Then remember the essentials of the Ephraim and Manasseh blessing, notice others' potential, call them by the right name, and point them to a positive future by God's grace. That's how easy it is to bless and empower the people you love.

Conclusion

The Best Is Yet to Come

Instead of exhorting people to make New Year's resolutions at our church, every January we bless all the people. After I explain that the Christian life isn't fueled by our vows to God but by His vows to us, I share a blessing that God inspires me to craft each New Year.[1] We then invite each individual or family to come forward, receive communion, and be blessed by a lay ministry team.

When we began this over twenty years ago, our church was smaller and it was easier to orchestrate. Now with four campuses and many more people, it's a logistical challenge to say the least. But we don't care, because when members of the body of Christ bless one another, beautiful things happen.

Can you imagine the scene? A grieving widow finds shelter under the assurances of blessing. A husband and wife whose marriage hangs by a thread hold hands and drink in the power of hope. A stressed-out young mother remembers how blessed she is. Expectant newlyweds discover a foundation of blessing upon which they can build their lives. An unemployed businessman is buoyed with confidence for his job search. Everywhere, people are melting with gratitude under the sound of blessing. Everyone leaves full—full of joy, full of hope. It seems a lot like heaven.

I might like New Year's Blessing Sunday more than Easter Sunday.

I know, of course, that normally it's best not to put church guests on the spot. It's better to give them personal space, allow them anonymity, and help them feel comfortable. But on New Year's Blessing Sunday, we overlook those commonly accepted principles of seeker sensitivity and invite people out of their pews and into a mystery.

I'd like to invite you to do the same. Grant me a most holy privilege. Will you open your heart and let me bless your life?

It's easy. You just have to act like a camel.

The Hebrew word for "bless" is the same word for "kneel": *barak*. Some scholars suggest that "kneel" and "bless" are the same word in Hebrew because, in ancient Middle Eastern culture, the giver of a gift would bow or kneel while presenting the gift. In one sense, a blessing is a gift that is given with a humble heart. But I once heard Hebrew scholar Dr. Karl Coke explain it differently.

In the ancient, arid Middle East, camels were treasures. They have a third clear eyelid that protects their eyes from sand, and they can survive without water for up to six months. And they can carry a surprising weight. Before a long journey, a camel might be loaded with goods, supplies, or treasures weighing up to nine hundred pounds. In order for someone to load up the camel, it had to kneel. The image of the kneeling camel receiving its valuable load, Dr. Coke has explained, is the likely origin of the word "bless."

To be blessed is to be loaded with the Master's treasures.

Camels can run up to forty miles per hour, but they have to stop and awkwardly kneel in order to be loaded. Will you be like a camel for a few moments, pause from your busy, important journey, kneel in the Spirit, and let me load you with the Master's goods?

I've shared some of my story. I've explained the principle and power of blessing. I've pointed you to a practical way to start blessing others. But before we part, here's what I most want to give you—my blessing.

A Parting Blessing

I write this blessing with confidence because it's filled with scriptural affirmations that are promises for every believer. If you're still exploring Christianity, there's much in my blessing for you too. It follows the outline of the four essential gifts of the Ephraim and Manasseh blessing. I didn't compose it as an overview or a theology of biblical blessing. It's more personal than that. Just take my words as they are, words of blessing from my heart to yours, spoken in faith and rooted in God's own Word.

"Ephraim and Manasseh Shall Be Mine": The Gift of Security

Beloved, you belong to God.

Before God's voice thundered into the unformed cosmos, sending forth light at 186,000 miles per second, before He created the Canis Majoris star large enough to house seven quadrillion earths, before He set the earth on its elliptical course and started it spinning, God imagined you. His eyes saw your "unformed substance," and your days were written in God's book "when as yet there was none of them" (Ps. 139:16). Before the Lord "formed you in the womb," He "knew you" (Jer. 1:5).

The pinnacle of God's creation is not seen in the expanse of the Grand Canyon or in the towering sequoias of the Redwood Forest. *You* are the pinnacle of God's handiwork. His greatest masterpiece is not unveiled in a multihued sunset over a rolling ocean or in a radiant rainbow arced across freshly emptied clouds. *You* are God's masterpiece.

God made you in His own image. You reflect His glory in the earth. He made you "a little lower than the angels and crowned [you] with glory and honor" (Ps. 8:5 NIV). He wove His majesty into the mysterious DNA hidden in each of your hundred trillion cells. You are unmatched.

No one else has your fingerprints. But more than the marvel of your physical complexity is the wonder of your soul—you're brimming with glorious, personal uniqueness. The way you laugh, the thoughts you imagine, your capacity to learn and love—your whole, complex, inmost being bears the image of God in this world.

You belong to God because He made you, but in Christ, there is much more. You're like the little boat that a boy loved to sail at the local lake. He'd made the boat with his own hands, and he loved it. One day a stiff wind overtook the toy vessel and blew it across the lake. The boy looked for his lost boat for weeks, until one day he saw it in the window of the local general store. He rushed to the store owner and breathlessly announced, "The boat in the window is mine!"

"I'm sorry," the owner said. "I paid someone for it. If you want it, you'll have to buy it."

The boy ran home, spilled open his piggy bank, and brought every coin he owned to the store. Seeing the lad's sacrificial commitment, the store owner sold the boat to the boy. As the child stepped onto the sidewalk, he held up his handcrafted treasure and declared, "Little boat, you're mine, you're mine. You're twice mine. You're mine because I made you and you're mine because I bought you."

In Christ, you're twice God's. You're His because He made you and you're His because He bought you. "You are not your own, for you were bought with a price" (1 Cor. 6:19–20). You "belong to Christ" (1 Cor. 3:23 NCV) because you were not purchased with "perishable things such as silver or gold, but with the precious blood of Christ" (1 Pet. 1:18–19). If an infinitely wealthy God paid His whole fortune for you, you must be endlessly valuable.

God has too much invested in you to ever let you go. He chose you in Christ before the foundation of the world. He predestined you "for adoption to himself" (Eph. 1:5). Once adopted as God's son or daughter, you cannot be disowned. If you were to "rise on the wings of the dawn . . . [and] settle on the far side of the sea" (Ps. 139:9 NIV), God would arrive before you in order to love you.

You're safe in the love of God. "You did not receive the spirit of slavery to fall back into fear, but you have received the Spirit of adoption" (Rom. 8:15). So fear no evil, beloved heir of God.

Whether your bank account is big or small, whether you are young or old, whether you are in the valley or on the mountaintop, in Christ, you're the heir of spiritual riches and assured of your place at the King's family table forever.

Child of God, live without fear. "For I am sure that neither death nor life, nor angels nor rulers, nor things present nor things to come, nor powers, nor height nor depth, nor anything else in all creation, will be able to separate [you] from the love of God in Christ Jesus our Lord" (Rom. 8:38–39).

As Manasseh: The Gift of Freedom

I bless you to be as Manasseh—whose name means "forgotten all my troubles"—that you will be so aware of God's grace right here, right now, that yesterday's woes will find no root in your heart today.

As the sun dawned upon the horizon this morning, this day came fresh to you, wholly new. You're alive for this moment. God's mercies are "new every morning" for you (Lam. 3:23). Yesterday's losses, regrets, disappointments, and failures cannot define you because God is an innovator, always making things new. "Remember not the former things, nor consider the things of old. Behold, I am doing a new thing; now it springs forth," says the Lord (Isa. 43:18–19).

You are defined not by the pain of the past but by the plans of God.

Though Joseph's first thirty years were riddled with sorrow and disappointment, God's triumphant, providential plan for Joseph eclipsed the adversities of Egypt. God has engineered such a plan for you.

He may not plan for you to help govern a nation like Joseph, but He has always intended for you to "reign in life through . . . Jesus Christ" (Rom. 5:17). You can forget what lies behind and "press on toward the goal for the prize of the upward call of God in Christ Jesus" (Phil. 3:14).

Yesterday is over, but the rubble of your past shall not be wasted. "This is what the LORD says: 'I will restore the fortunes of Jacob's tents and have compassion on his dwellings; the city will be rebuilt on her ruins'" (Jer. 30:18 NIV). God is not blind to your losses. He is not deaf to your cries. He is moved with unquenchable compassion on your behalf. He is a restorer, a master renovator, who can incorporate every broken fragment of yesteryear into the foundation of a new, higher place for you to dwell. Like the ancient cities rebuilt upon the ruins of former days, your adversities have become clay in God's hands—He's molding a mountain out of your mistakes so you can live atop it all with a whole new perspective.

No matter what voices of shame have hellishly plagued you, no matter how persistent the inward, gnawing guilt, "there is therefore now no condemnation for those who are in Christ Jesus" (Rom. 8:1). When you trust in Christ, you're fully, forever forgiven. If you've never asked God for His forgiveness, when you ask Him now, He promises to hold no sin against you.

He will never dredge up the past to shame you. By His own sovereign choice, the Lord remembers your sin no more (Jer. 31:34). He has removed your trespasses from you as far as the east is from the west (Ps. 103:12). Christ has paid for your sin in full. So God, in His righteousness, will never require your payment for a debt that has already been cleared.

Beloved, you are Manasseh. The troubles of the past do not define you—they refine you. In Christ, you are not bound by the rubble of the past—you are lifted higher. Today is the first day of the rest of your life!

As Ephraim: The Gift of Fruitfulness

I bless you to be as Ephraim, whose name means "twice fruitful." Joseph's secondborn son proved that God not only delights in redeeming the past but also takes joy in making His beloved more productive than ever imagined.

God blessed your earliest ancestors to "be fruitful and multiply and fill the earth and subdue it, and have dominion" (Gen. 1:28), and His will has not changed. He has likewise destined you to "bear much fruit" (John 15:8). You're a sower, a spiritual farmer, whose harvest will come in due season. I bless the seed you have in the ground. May all your good, hard work sprout and grow into sweet fruit containing more seed. I bless the seed you have in your hand—the good intentions and investments of your life that you are now scattering. Remember, the smallest seed can grow into the greatest, most fruitful tree.

I bless you to "prosper in all things and be in health, just as your soul prospers" (3 John v. 2 NKJV). May you prosper in "*all* things"—your relationships, your parenting, your vocation, your ministry, your creativity, your finances, your prayer life, your wisdom for planning, your capacity to love. Flourish. Grow. Bear much fruit.

I bless you to find energy for your work through your sense of destiny. God has woven unique gifts and aspirations into the fabric of your life that position you for a role that no one else can fill, whether at home or in the workplace. You are God's "workmanship, created in Christ Jesus for good works, which God prepared beforehand" (Eph. 2:10).

May your heart be increasingly filled with the fruit of the Spirit: love, joy, peace, patience, kindness, goodness, faithfulness, gentleness, and self-control (Gal. 5:22–23). I bless your patience in times of suffering and your faith in the seasons of sowing. I bless the spiritual thirst in your inmost being to keep drawing you ever nearer to God, and I bless your mind to think on whatever is true, noble, right, pure, lovely, admirable, excellent, and praiseworthy (Phil. 4:8).

If God's adopting love has been set upon you from eternity and He is fully able to redeem every event of your life, then it must be possible for Him to work in and through you to do "far more than you could ever imagine or guess or request in your wildest dreams" (Eph. 3:20 Message).

Crossing His Hands: The Gift of Favor

As Jesus, "the firstborn of all creation" (Col. 1:15), slowly suffocated on a Roman cross, the Father did the unimaginable. He took His strong right hand of blessing from the firstborn's bleeding head and moved it toward the head of the undeserving younger siblings—you and me.

God crossed His arms in grace.

Not only does being in Christ mean that you are secure in God's love, free from the past, and destined to bear much fruit, but it also means that you can walk in the favor of God—a blessing that should have rested on the sinless Savior alone. God died in your place so that He could regard you as if you were as pure and meritorious as Jesus.

With such a gift in mind, there is no limit to the favor of God on your life.

Therefore, child of grace, I bless you to live all your days under the right hand of God's favor. When times are hard, may God create a way in the wilderness for you. When times are dry, may He provide rivers in the desert for you (Isa. 43:19). When times are uncertain, may God cover you "with favor as with a shield" (Ps. 5:12). When it's time for work, may "the favor of the Lord our God be upon [you], and establish the work of [your] hands" (Ps. 90:17). In all of life, may you grow in wisdom, stature, and favor with God and people everywhere (Luke 2:52).

When you live according to the law, you get only what you earn. But you, adopted child, are no longer under the law (Rom. 6:14). You are under the right hand of grace. As such, the best things in your life are and always will be unearned. Unmerited. Free. Unexpected. Better than you could acquire by human effort.

Beloved, in Christ, you are fully qualified "to share in the inheritance of the saints" (Col. 1:12). As such, none of your weaknesses or faults can disqualify you from the favor of God, and no other person should be more expectant of the favor of God than you. Because with God all things are possible (Matt. 19:26), you can do all things through Christ who strengthens you (Phil. 4:13).

You're under His favor during the night and during the day, in the storm and in the calm. Whether you feel it now or not, His right hand rests upon you. Whether you see it or not, the grace of God goes before you. I bless you to live with constant expectancy for God to open doors of opportunity for you. You are made to thrive by His grace, not strive under the law. May the joy of the Lord be your strength in the dark so you'll be found dancing when the spotlight hits you.

In all these ways and more, may God make you as Ephraim and Manasseh.

Amen.

The Best Is Yet to Come

My wife, Anne, always had a special love for her grandmother, Mama Bennett, the matriarch of the Bennett clan. Mama Bennett bore six sons (one was Stanley, whom I introduced you to earlier) and two daughters and raised them in the small town of York, South Carolina, where her husband, C.P., was the police chief. Bonnie, my mother-in-law, was the youngest. Though her brothers occasionally used little Bonnie as a human football, her dearest, earliest memories were all connected to that old house in York.

Bonnie lived a full life, but Alzheimer's untimely theft began when she was in her seventies. In the early days of her dementia and decline, she would beg my father-in-law to take her home to York. Dozens of times, Graham patiently drove Bonnie the one hundred miles from Winston-Salem, North Carolina, to York, and each time, Bonnie would discover that her family was no longer there.

Bonnie was confused, but she wanted what we all want—she wanted to go home.

Anne remembers that house in York from the yearly gatherings there on Christmas nights. All the aunts and uncles would come—Orin and Rossie, Vera and Max, Joe, Bill and Barbara, Charlie and Martha, Stanley and Joella, Duddy and Jane, and the kids. What a big band of cousins.

The York house had no air-conditioning but was wrapped with a classic, expansive front porch where the big, happy family rocked and laughed and told stories and ate peach cobbler. When it was time to open presents, the kids and adults would cram into Mama Bennett's big living room and, in a flurry of bows and paper, tear into the gifts and run about hugging and kissing and thanking each other.

Love. Security. Joy. Memory. It was all there at the old York house on Christmas night.

Last Thanksgiving, after six and a half years in the dementia care facility, my sweet mother-in-law became unresponsive, and we knew it wouldn't be long before she flew away from this earth. As a pastor I've seen it more times than I can remember. A family vigil of around-the-clock care began. Bonnie was unconscious, her breathing labored, but she lingered for days.

On the third night, as Anne was returning to the care facility, the Lord visited her with a vision. A beautiful, blissful scene welled up in her spirit. Suddenly, Anne saw herself on the sofa in Mama Bennett's big living room on Christmas night. She was surrounded by the aunts and uncles she loved so much. The big living room was echoing with their laughter once again. All the siblings but Bonnie and her brother Duddy had died long before. So in a flash, Anne realized that God was showing her more than a memory—He was showing her a portrait of heaven. God was revealing what awaited Bonnie.

Profoundly nourished by the vision, Anne arrived to continue the holy vigil. Several of us were there. Anne sat on the corner of the bed and began to bless her unresponsive mother.

"Mom," she said, "I believe I had a vision of what it will be like when you arrive in heaven. Remember what it was like at Mama Bennett's on Christmas night? It's going to be like stepping off her front porch into that big living room where all your family is gathered. They're all there, Mom— your dad and Mama Bennett and Orin and Vera and Bill and Charlie and Joe and Stanley. Everyone's there, catching up, laughing over warm, rich memories. The Christmas lights are twinkling, and the food is hot on the table. Everyone's hugging. That's what heaven is going to be like for you, Mom. You're going to step off Mama Bennett's porch into the middle of all that joy."

As Anne was describing it all, for the first time in many days, Bonnie opened her eyes and tried to speak. I think she saw what Anne saw.

We gathered close to her and began singing "Amazing Grace," and with a final exhale, Bonnie stepped off the porch into heaven.

My wife had assumed the vision was for her, but she realized it was for her mother. It was God's plan to bring Bonnie into glory by the power of blessing.

I've watched blessing at work for twenty-five years, but that day I saw something I'd never seen: I watched the power of blessing take a saint home.

When a loved one is at their weakest and we feel utterly impotent, we still have the power to bless. I've come to realize that it's God's plan to bring us into this world under the sound of blessing and to take us home under the same sweet sound.

I spent too many of my years living like Jacob—striving or pretending in an effort to garner favor and feel blessed.

That's why I came to love the old patriarch. I'll never tire of his stories. I'll never stop reading and preaching Jacob's unsettling tales, because seeing myself in Jacob became my liberation.

I saw in Jacob the futility of trying to earn what can only be given. I saw my own striving heart in his, and I wanted something different. Those crossed hands of Jacob led me to the crossed hands of the Father, where I saw more clearly than ever the magnificence of the exchange that has taken place on the cross for you and for me.

There, in those crossed hands, I saw more clearly and believed more deeply than ever before that I could be blessed because Christ had taken my place and given me His. I thank God that I didn't have to wait until my deathbed, like Jacob, to understand the power of blessing.

I'm so thankful that God taught me the power to bless while I still had time to do it. There's time for you too—you can start today.

Find someone you love and say, "May God make you as Ephraim and Manasseh." When they say, "What do you mean?" you'll realize that you have a story to tell and that you have been given the power to bless.

Appendix A

Simple, Powerful Blessings from the Bible

Scriptural Blessings to Affirm Security

On Being Secure as a Child of God

"[Name], you did not receive the spirit of slavery to fall back into fear, but you have received the Spirit of adoption as sons, by whom we cry, 'Abba! Father!' The Spirit himself bears witness with your spirit that you are a child of God, and if a child, then an heir—an heir of God and fellow heir with Christ." (Rom. 8:15–17)

SEE ALSO:

Psalm 68:5–6; Romans 8:29; 2 Corinthians 6:18; Galatians 3:26; 4:6–7; Ephesians 1:4–6; 1 John 3:1

On Being Safe in God's Love

"[Name], I am sure that neither death nor life, nor angels nor rulers, nor things present nor things to come, nor powers, nor height nor depth, nor anything else in all creation, will be able

to separate you from the love of God in Christ Jesus our Lord."
(Rom. 8:38–39)

SEE ALSO:

Psalms 23:1–3; 46:1–3; 121:3–4; John 10:28–29; 2 Timothy 1:12;
1 John 3:1

On Living without Fear

"[Name], no weapon that is fashioned against you shall succeed.
God has not given you a spirit of fear, but of love, power, and a
sound mind." (Isa. 54:17 and 2 Tim. 1:7)

SEE ALSO:

Psalms 91:9–12; 118:6; John 14:27; Philippians 4:7; 1 John 4:17

Scriptural Blessings to Affirm Freedom

On Assurance of God's Forgiveness

"[Name], God has removed your sins from you as far as the east
is from the west. They are gone, and He remembers them no
more!" (Ps. 103:12 and Isa. 43:25)

SEE ALSO:

Isaiah 1:18; Matthew 26:27–28; Romans 6:6, 11; 8:1; Ephesians 1:7;
Colossians 1:13–14

On God's Heart to Restore

"[Name], the Lord has good plans in store for you—plans for
your welfare and not for evil, to give you a future and a hope."
(Jer. 29:11)

SEE ALSO:

Psalms 23:3; 51:12; Isaiah 61:7; Acts 3:20–21; 1 Peter 5:10

On Freedom in Christ

"[Name], you can know the truth, and the truth will set you free." (John 8:32)

SEE ALSO:

Isaiah 61:1; Romans 8:2; 2 Corinthians 3:17; Galatians 5:1; Hebrews 2:14–15

Scriptural Blessings to Affirm Fruitfulness

On Bearing the Fruit of the Spirit

"[Name], because you have the Holy Spirit in your heart, you are destined to bear the fruit of the Spirit: love, joy, peace, patience, kindness, goodness, faithfulness, gentleness, self-control; against such things there is no law." (Gal. 5:22–23)

SEE ALSO:

Nehemiah 8:10; Psalm 30:5; Romans 5:1; 15:13; Ephesians 3:14–19; James 1:2–3; 1 Peter 1:8; 1 John 4:16, 19

On Being Productive

"[Name], God is at work in you, and He can do far more abundantly than all that you ask or think, according to the power at work within you!" (Eph. 3:20)

SEE ALSO:

Genesis 1:28; Deuteronomy 28:8; Proverbs 16:3; Acts 20:35; 2 Corinthians 9:6; Ephesians 2:10

On Prospering/Flourishing

"[Name], God has made you to be like a tree planted by streams of water that yields its fruit in its season, and its leaf does not wither. In all that you do, may you prosper." (Ps. 1:3)

SEE ALSO:

Genesis 39:23; 1 Samuel 18:14; Psalms 103:2–5; 115:14–15; Luke 6:38; John 10:10; Romans 5:17; 2 Corinthians 9:8; Philippians 4:19–20; James 1:17; 3 John v. 2

Scriptural Blessings to Affirm Favor

On God's Heart to Show Favor

"[Name], the Lord God is a sun and shield for you; the Lord bestows favor and honor upon you." (Ps. 84:11)

SEE ALSO:

Genesis 6:8; Exodus 33:17; Psalms 5:12; 30:5; Proverbs 22:1; Luke 1:30; 4:18–19; Acts 7:45–46

On Finding Favor with People or Opportunities

"[Name], as Jesus did, may you increase in wisdom and in stature and in favor with God and man." (Luke 2:52)

SEE ALSO:

1 Samuel 2:26; Nehemiah 1:11; Esther 2:17; Psalm 90:17; Proverbs 3:4; Isaiah 43:19; Daniel 1:9; Acts 2:46–47

On the Christian's New, Favored Position in Christ

"[Name], God has blessed you in Christ with every spiritual blessing in the heavenly places." (Eph. 1:3)

SEE ALSO:

John 1:16; 1 Corinthians 12:12–13; Ephesians 1:18–19; 2:5–6; 3:20–21; 4:7–8; Hebrews 4:16

Blessings for Every Season

Below is a sampling of blessings I've spoken over my congregation during the past two decades.

A Conqueror's Blessing
for a Season of Spiritual Battle

(based on Josh. 1)

Get ready to cross the Jordan into the land that I am about to give you. I will give you every place that you set your foot. No one will be able to stand up against you all the days of your life.

As I was with Moses, so I will be with you; I will never leave you nor forsake you. Be strong and courageous, because you will lead these people to inherit the land.

Be careful to obey all the law my servant Moses gave you; do not turn from it to the right or left, that you may be successful wherever you go. Do not let this Book of the Law depart from your mouth; meditate on it day and night, so that you may be careful to do everything written in it. Then you will be prosperous and successful.

A Restoration Blessing for Seasons of Loss

(Jer. 30:18–19 NIV)

This is what the Lord says: "I will restore the fortunes of Jacob's tents and have compassion on his dwellings; the city will be rebuilt on her ruins, and the palace will stand in its proper place. From them will come songs of thanksgiving and the sound of rejoicing. I will add to their numbers, and they will not be decreased; I will bring them honor, and they will not be disdained."

An Expectancy Blessing for a Season of New Endeavors

(based on Eph. 3:2–21)

Beloved, in Jesus Christ, you're blessed beyond what your mind can now conceive. In that sense, you are blessed beyond belief!

God is at work in you and through you and for you in ways that are exceedingly, abundantly above all you can currently ask or think. Therefore, I believe this is a season for your vision of God's glory to grow, your experience of God's greatness to grow, and your assurance of God's goodness to grow.

A Contentment Blessing
for a Season of Fresh Vision

(based on Ps. 17:15)

I bless you that, in the coming season, you'll have a fresh,
transforming vision of Jesus Christ.
May you know yourself to be the righteousness of Christ
through His cross. May you boldly draw near to Him and
behold His face, smiling upon you.
As you awake each day this season, may your life be full and
satisfied by simply seeing who Jesus is and what He has
done for you.

A Favor Blessing for a Season of Uncertainty

(based on Dan. 2:27, 47; 3:25; 6:22)

As you move expectantly into this new season, may the Lord
protect you, provide for you, and promote you as He did
Daniel.
May God's grace protect you in the midst of the fiery furnace
and shut the mouth of the roaring lion. You can dare to stay
true to God because in Christ, you are safe.
May God's grace provide you with supernatural wisdom, revelation, and direction amid the world's confusion. You can
see the right path because in Christ, you are discerning.
May God's grace promote you in surprising ways. You can
bless the world while bringing glory to God because in
Christ, you are favored.

The Red Sea Blessing for a Season of Obstacles

(based on Exod. 14:13–14 NKJV)

When you've experienced God's freedom and favor but find yourself facing new, unexpected challenges, take heart. God still parts Red Seas. Receive the word Moses gave the Israelites when they felt trapped between an army behind and an ocean in front:

"Do not be afraid. Stand still, and see the salvation of the Lord, which He will accomplish for you today. For the Egyptians whom you see today, you shall see again no more forever. The Lord will fight for you, and you shall hold your peace."

The Peter Blessing for a Season of New Mission

(based on Matt. 16:15–19)

Blessed are you, for God reveals spiritual treasures to you that flesh and blood cannot discern. I bless you to see more of who Jesus is, so that you'll see more of who you are in Christ.

- You're a rock—a living stone in God's unstoppable church.
- You're a victor—the gates of hell cannot prevail against you.
- You're a key bearer—filled with the grace of God that opens heaven's doors.
- You're a representative of God—bold with spiritual authority in the earth.

The Elijah Blessing for a Season
of Spiritual or Emotional Drought

(based on 1 Kings 18:41–44 and James 5:16–18)

There is the sound of the rushing of rain—may your ears be
blessed to hear it. There is a miraculous outpouring on the
horizon—may your eyes be blessed to see it.
If you are in a season of drought, take heart. A small cloud
rises from the sea of God's grace. If you are in a season of
plenty, praise Him. God's grace knows no bounds.
Elijah was just as human as you are, and God changed the
whole atmosphere through his prayers. Likewise, your
prayers are unspeakably powerful and effective because when you are in Christ, you are clothed with His
righteousness.
May the heavens open and miracles rain down this year, bringing glory to God and blessing to many, in Jesus's name.

The Savor Blessing for a Season of Mindfulness

(based on Isa. 43:16–19 NIV)

Yesterday, with its joys and sorrows, is over. Tomorrow, with
its hopes and challenges, is yet to exist. But today, right
here, right now, God's grace blooms before your very eyes.
This is what the Lord says through Isaiah:

"Forget the former things;
Do not dwell on the past.
See, I am doing a new thing!
Now it springs up."

Led by the Spirit, you can become mindful of every blessing
and savor the textures and flavors of God's grace, each moment, in the moment, every day this year.

A New Vision Blessing
for a Season of Blurred Perspective

(based on John 1:50–51)

May God give you the eyes of Jesus, so you'll see everything
as He sees it. Through Christ's eyes, as He promised Na-
thanael, "you'll see greater things" this season.
Under a cloudless, open heaven, may you have the Savior's
own clear vision so that

- you'll see yourself more beloved than broken
- you'll see others' potential more than their problems
- you'll see the world's hope more than its heartaches

God's grace is all around you. You'll see.

Notes

Introduction: The Blessing I Never Knew

1. Dallas Willard, *Living in Christ's Presence: Final Words on Heaven and the Kingdom of God* (Downers Grove, IL: InterVarsity Press, 2014), 164.

Chapter 1 The Problem of the Unblessed Life

1. Marilyn Monroe, *My Story* (New York: Taylor Trade, 2007), 4.

2. Monroe, 5.

3. Sam Kashner, "Marilyn and Her Monsters," *Vanity Fair*, October 5, 2010, www.vanityfair.com/culture/2010/11/marilyn-monroe-201011.

4. Sean Alfano, "The Lonely States of America," CBS News, June 28, 2006, www.cbsnews.com/news/the-lonely-states-of-america.

5. Alfano, "The Lonely States of America."

6. HRSA, Health Resources & Services Administration, "The Loneliness Epidemic," January 2019, www.hrsa.gov/enews/past-issues/2019/january-17/loneliness-epidemic.

7. A UCLA study demonstrated that feelings of rejection and isolation affect the brain in similar ways to physical pain. See Veronique de Turenne, "The Pain of Chronic Loneliness Can Be Detrimental to Your Health," UCLA Newsroom, December 21, 2016, newsroom.ucla.edu/stories/stories-20161206.

8. Dan Kiley, *The Peter Pan Syndrome: Men Who Have Never Grown Up* (New York: Dodd Mead, 1983).

9. Michael Hyatt and Daniel Harkavy, *Living Forward: A Proven Plan to Stop Drifting and Get the Life You Want* (Grand Rapids: Baker Books, 2016), 30.

10. "The Villain and the Showgirl: A Closer Look at Arthur Miller and Marilyn Monroe," Immortal Marilyn, November 15, 2015, https:// www.immortalmarilyn.com/the-villain-and-the-showgirl-a-closer -look-at-arthur-miller-and-marilyn-monroe/.

11. Kashner, "Marilyn and Her Monsters."

Chapter 2 Why Blessing Precedes Success

1. "Believe in U.S.: Julia Mancuso," U.S. Ski & Snowboard, November 29, 2013, https://usskiandsnowboard.org/news/believe-us-julia-man cuso.

2. Wikipedia, s.v. "Julia Mancuso," last modified February 22, 2020, 22:25, https://en.wikipedia.org/wiki/Julia_Mancuso#cite_note-team usa-1.

3. Dani Cooper, "Risky Teens Are Fatalistic: Study," ABC Science, July 2, 2009, https://www.abc.net.au/science/articles/2009/07/02/261 5039.htm.

4. Katherine Ellison, "Being Honest about the Pygmalion Effect," *Discover*, October 29, 2015, http://discovermagazine.com/2015/dec/14 -great-expectations.

5. Malcolm Gladwell, *Blink* (New York: Little, Brown and Company, 2007), 56.

Chapter 3 If You Can See It, You Can Be It

1. John Calvin, *Institutes of the Christian Religion*, trans. Henry Beveridge (Bellingham, WA: Logos Research Systems, Inc., 2010), 64. Here's the full reference: "For as the aged, or those whose sight is defective, when any book, however fair, is set before them, though they perceive that there is something written, are scarcely able to make out two consecutive words, but, when aided by glasses, begin to read distinctly, so Scripture, gathering together the impressions of Deity, which, till then, lay confused in our minds, dissipates the darkness, and shows us the true God clearly."

2. See www.purposebuiltcommunities.org for more info.

Chapter 4 Blessed to Be Secure

1. Martin Luther King Jr., "Martin Luther King Jr. Speaks with NBC News 11 Months before Assassination," interview by Sander Vanocur,

16:46–52, https://nbcpalmsprings.com/2019/01/15/martin-luther-king
-jr-speaks-with-nbc-news-11-months-before-assassination/.

Chapter 5 Blessed to Be Free

1. Brené Brown, *I Thought It Was Just Me (but It Isn't): Making the Journey from "What Will People Think?" to "I Am Enough"* (New York: Gotham Books, 2007), loc. 826 of 5267, Kindle.

Chapter 6 Blessed to Be Twice Fruitful

1. Ian Tully, "Situationism and Virtue Ethics," 1000-Word Philosophy, March 10, 2014, https://1000wordphilosophy.com/2014/03/10/situationism-and-virtue-ethics.

2. Dudley Hall, *Grace Works: Rescued from Senseless Rebellion and Lifeless Religion*, updated ed. (Euless, TX: Kerygma Ventures Press, 2013), loc. 2366 of 3753, Kindle.

3. Malcolm Gladwell, *What the Dog Saw: And Other Adventures* (New York: Little, Brown and Company, 2009), 263.

4. John Wesley, *John Wesley*, ed. Albert C. Outler (New York: Oxford University Press, 1964), 245.

5. Charles Wallace Jr., ed., *Susanna Wesley: The Complete Writings* (Oxford: Oxford University Press, 1997), 64.

6. Timothy Keller, *Walking with God through Pain and Suffering* (New York: Riverhead Books, 2013), 266.

Chapter 7 Blessed to Be Favored

1. The literal translation of Augustine's famous quote is, "New Testament in the Old lies, the Old Testament in the New is clear." Augustine, *Questions on the Heptateuch* 2, 73: PL 34, 623.

2. Grant Wacker, "Watershed: Los Angeles 1949," *Christian History* 111, 2014, https://christianhistoryinstitute.org/magazine/article/watershed-los-angeles-1949.

Chapter 8 Why Blessing Works

1. John Trent, Gary Smalley, and Kari Trent Stageberg, *The Blessing: Giving the Gift of Unconditional Love and Acceptance* (Nashville: Thomas Nelson, 2019), 115.

2. Martin Luther King Jr., "I Have a Dream" (speech, Lincoln Memorial, Washington, DC, August 28, 1963).

3. Lera Boroditsky, "Lost in Translation," *Wall Street Journal*, July 23, 2010, https://www.wsj.com/articles/SB10001424052748703467304575383131592767868.

4. Helen Keller, *My Religion* (New York: Doubleday, 1927), 20–21.

5. Wyatt Turbeville, "24-Year-Old wins $768.4 Million Powerball Jackpot," WCJB (ABC), April 24, 2019, https://www.wcjb.com/content/news/24-year-old-wins-7684-Million-Powerball-jackpot-508993711.html.

6. Dudley Hall, "Naming the Animals," Successful Christian Living Ministries, February 2007, PDF.

7. Carolyn Y. Johnson, "Nobel Prize in Medicine Awarded for Discovery of How Cells Sense Oxygen," *Washington Post*, October 7, 2019, https://www.washingtonpost.com/science/2019/10/07/nobel-prize-medicine-awarded-discovery-how-cells-sense-oxygen/.

Chapter 9 Blessing Your Own Life

1. Charlie W. Shedd, *Letters to Philip* (Garden City, NY: Doubleday & Company, 1968), 17–18.

2. C. S. Lewis, *Mere Christianity* (New York: HarperCollins, 2009), 128.

3. Timothy Keller, *The Freedom of Self-Forgetfulness: The Path to True Christian Joy* (LaGrange, KY: 10Publishing, 2012), loc. 126 of 431, Kindle.

Chapter 10 Learning to Speak Like God

1. Timothy Keller, "The Problem of Blessing," October 28, 2001, in *Gospel in Life*, produced by Timothy J. Keller, MP3 audio, 13:24–28, https://gospelinlife.com/downloads/the-problem-of-blessing-5247/.

2. Andrea Alfano, "Too Much Praise Promotes Narcissism," *Scientific American*, June 1, 2015, https://www.scientificamerican.com/article/too-much-praise-promotes-narcissism/.

3. Thanks to Dr. Bill Satterwhite for sharing this diagram with me. It was envisioned and designed by another mutual friend, Don Flow.

4. John Steinbeck, *East of Eden* (New York: Penguin Books, 2002), 477.

5. Timothy Keller, *The Prodigal God* (New York: Dutton, 2008), 29.

6. Keller, *The Prodigal God*, 31.

Chapter 11 You Can Learn to Bless Anyone

1. Bob Goff, *Everybody, Always: Becoming Love in a World Full of Setbacks and Difficult People* (Nashville: Nelson Books, 2018), 29.

2. Martin Luther, quoted in Don Kistler, ed., *Let Us Pray: A Symposium on Prayer by Leading Preachers and Theologians* (Orlando: Northampton Press, 2011), loc. 1484 of 4131, Kindle.

3. Brené Brown, *I Thought It Was Just Me*, loc. 815 of 5265, Kindle.

4. Gary Smalley and John Trent, *The Gift of the Blessing* (Nashville: Thomas Nelson, 1993), 99.

5. Smalley and Trent, *Gift of the Blessing*, 103.

Blessing Worksheet

1. As Smalley and Trent describe, most biblical blessing includes physical touch. See *The Gift of the Blessing*, pages 11ff., for their discussion of the importance of physical touch. It is essential to discern a recipient's comfort level with physical touch. Be considerate of the recipient's demeanor. People are designed for touch and physical affection—it is essential for human health. However, blessing is powerful with or without physical touch.

Conclusion The Best Is Yet to Come

1. See appendix B for examples of New Year's blessings that I've modified for use in a variety of seasons.

In addition to leading a historic, dynamic multisite congregation in North Carolina, **Alan Wright** is a five-time author, popular conference speaker, and radio teacher whose message of life-empowering grace is heard on four hundred stations across the nation. Alan also hosts a weekly podcast and sends an inspiring devotional to tens of thousands of subscribers every day.

Alan and Anne have been married for thirty-five years. Their son, Bennett (married to Amy), is a Duke Law graduate, and their daughter, Abby, is a senior at the University of North Carolina at Chapel Hill.

Alan loves golf, piano, and dating his wife every week. Anne loves to make people laugh and leads Awakenings, a Bible study reaching hundreds of women every week. For more about Alan Wright Ministries, visit www.pastor alan.org.

ALAN WRIGHT MINISTRIES
See Your Life in a Whole New Light

WHO ARE YOU REALLY? It's time to find out! Join the AWM community, where you can discover and embrace your true identity in Christ. Today is the day you can begin seeing your life in a whole new light. Visit pastoralan.org to get free resources, including

- **Daily devotions and emails from Pastor Alan**
- **Podcasts**
- **Pastor Alan's daily radio broadcast**
- **Mobile content**
- **Information on events and conferences**

And many more resources that will bless and encourage you!

pastoralan.org

THE
POWER TO
BLESS
audiobook

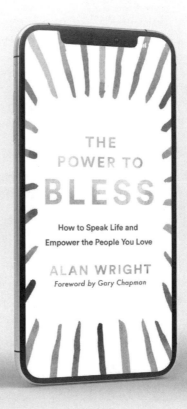

THE
POWER TO
BLESS

How to Speak Life and
Empower the People You Love

ALAN WRIGHT
Foreword by Gary Chapman

**Available on all major platforms,
including Audible and Apple**

THE
BLESSING
PODCAST

Fill your life with the power of blessing by subscribing to Pastor Alan's *Blessing* podcast.

You'll receive regular, powerful, biblically based blessings that you can appropriate and then share with others to bless their lives!

pastoralan.org

THE
POWER TO
BLESS

s e m i n a r

Don't just read about the power of blessing—experience it firsthand!

The Power to Bless comes to life in this two-hour learning experience with Pastor Alan Wright.

Participants discover the power of biblical blessing up close with Pastor Alan. It's a time to laugh, learn, and leave with all the practical tools needed to speak life and empower the people we love.

**Contact us at pastoralan.org
to schedule for your church
or ministry venue.**

ARE YOU READY FOR SOME GOOD NEWS?

GET THE FREE DAILY DEVOTIONAL!

Start your day with inspiration from God's Word as Pastor Alan explores a variety of nourishing topics every weekday.

pastoralan.org

DAILY RADIO BROADCAST

Whether you are at home or on the go, you can be nourished by this daily, thirty-minute sermon broadcast heard on 400 stations nationwide and available everywhere via podcast.

Tune in or find a station near you at pastoralan.org

INSIDE GRACE
WITH ALAN WRIGHT

An engaging podcast that invites you to take a deeper dive into the powerful, practical, life-changing dynamics of grace each week as Pastor Alan joins host Dr. Chris Lawson for uncommon conversations about the gospel and real life.

pastoralan.org

THE POWER OF BLESSING

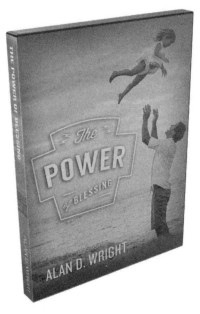

SHAME OFF YOU
CONFERENCE

Isn't it time you shed performance-based living?

It's time to walk away from shame! Laugh, learn, and find freedom as Pastor Alan invites you to discover your true identity in Christ, shed performance-based living, break unhealthy relationship habits, and get the shame off you for good!

Contact us at pastoralan.org to schedule for your church or ministry venue!

GOOD NEWS FOR PARENTS

CONFERENCE

**You can have a low-pressure,
high-expectation home . . . by God's grace**

You can learn how to motivate your kids the way God motivates *His* children. Join Pastor Alan and his wife, Anne, as they blend humor, deep gospel insights, and loads of practical advice to equip parents to raise their children in homes filled with grace and blessing.

Contact us at pastoralan.org to find out more!

GOOD NEWS FOR YOUR MARRIAGE

CONFERENCE

Marriages, like people, aren't changed by human effort; they're transformed by the gospel of grace. Join Pastor Alan and his wife, Anne, for an event that will lead husbands and wives into soul-nourishing, heart-thrilling insights that show a new way of living. This revolutionary way of approaching marriage—focusing on Christ's provision rather than your own efforts—will transform your relationship!

Contact us at pastoralan.org